COUNCIL *on* FOREIGN RELATIONS

I0026647

Discussion Paper
October 2019

The Security Implications of Human Trafficking

Jamille Bigio and Rachel Vogelstein

The Council on Foreign Relations (CFR) is an independent, nonpartisan membership organization, think tank, and publisher dedicated to being a resource for its members, government officials, business executives, journalists, educators and students, civic and religious leaders, and other interested citizens in order to help them better understand the world and the foreign policy choices facing the United States and other countries. Founded in 1921, CFR carries out its mission by maintaining a diverse membership, including special programs to promote interest and develop expertise in the next generation of foreign policy leaders; convening meetings at its headquarters in New York and in Washington, DC, and other cities where senior government officials, members of Congress, global leaders, and prominent thinkers come together with CFR members to discuss and debate major international issues; supporting a Studies Program that fosters independent research, enabling CFR scholars to produce articles, reports, and books and hold roundtables that analyze foreign policy issues and make concrete policy recommendations; publishing *Foreign Affairs*, the preeminent journal of international affairs and U.S. foreign policy; sponsoring Independent Task Forces that produce reports with both findings and policy prescriptions on the most important foreign policy topics; and providing up-to-date information and analysis about world events and American foreign policy on its website, CFR.org.

The Council on Foreign Relations takes no institutional positions on policy issues and has no affiliation with the U.S. government. All views expressed in its publications and on its website are the sole responsibility of the author or authors.

For further information about CFR or this paper, please write to the Council on Foreign Relations, 58 East 68th Street, New York, NY 10065, or call Communications at 212.434.9888. Visit CFR's website, CFR.org.

Copyright © 2019 by the Council on Foreign Relations®, Inc. All rights reserved.

This paper may not be reproduced in whole or in part, in any form beyond the reproduction permitted by Sections 107 and 108 of the U.S. Copyright Law Act (17 U.S.C. Sections 107 and 108) and excerpts by reviewers for the public press, without express written permission from the Council on Foreign Relations.

CONTENTS

INTRODUCTION

Human trafficking is a gross violation of human rights that affects populations across regional, ethnic, and religious lines. It encompasses a range of illicit activity, including sexual exploitation, forced labor, organ removal, and forcible recruitment into an armed group or military service. In 2016 alone, the United Nations detected close to twenty-five thousand victims of human trafficking, though this figure hides many unreported cases.[1] Seventy-two percent of them were women and girls. Globally, an estimated 40.3 million people in 2016 were entrapped in modern slavery—exploitative situations they could not leave or refuse due to coercion, deception, threats, or violence.[2]

But human trafficking is not only an affront to human rights and dignity—it is also a criminal and security concern. Human trafficking can fuel conflict by enabling armed and extremist groups to raise revenue and expand their power and military capabilities.[3] Human trafficking can also drive displacement and destabilize communities, thereby exacerbating conflict and undermining development.[4] When committed by security forces and peacekeepers, human trafficking undercuts the ability of international institutions to carry out their missions of promoting peace and stability.[5]

Forced labor produces an estimated $150 billion annually, making it one of the world's most profitable crimes.[6] It is also a funding mechanism for violent extremist organizations: groups such as the self-proclaimed Islamic State in Iraq and Syria and Boko Haram in Nigeria have enslaved women and girls and generated revenue from sex trafficking.[7] Governments may profit as well: state-sponsored trafficking can provide corrupt regimes a source of income and bolster their military capabilities.[8]

Despite the security implications of human trafficking, convictions for trafficking offenses are rare, programs focused on prevention and protection are under-resourced, and most efforts to address human trafficking are detached from broader conflict-prevention, security, and counterterrorism initiatives. To prevent human trafficking and advance U.S. security interests, the Donald J. Trump administration should use sanctions to apply a travel ban and asset freeze on human traffickers; pursue charges against Islamic State affiliates of sexual slavery and other forms of human trafficking; encourage troop-contributing countries to hold accountable peacekeepers who perpetrate sexual exploitation; collect intelligence on human trafficking in locations where it already tracks drug and arms trafficking; and lead by example by ensuring that its policies on migration and asylum disincentivize trafficking and support its victims. These steps will help the United States and its allies reduce human trafficking in conflict and terrorism-affected contexts while promoting broader peace and stability.

UNDERSTANDING HUMAN TRAFFICKING IN CONFLICT

Human trafficking occurs in almost every country in the world, but it takes on particularly abhorrent dimensions during and after conflict.[9] It is defined as the recruitment, transportation, transfer, harboring, or receipt of people through the threat or use of abduction, abuse of power or vulnerability, deception, coercion, fraud, force, or giving payments or benefits to a person in control of the victim for the purpose of exploitation.[10] While many trafficking victims are exploited within their countries of residence, other victims are trafficked across regions (see figure 1).

More than 72 percent of detected victims are women and girls; Western and Central Europe and North America, Central America, and the Caribbean have particularly high rates of detected women and girls (see figure 2).

Some forms of trafficking are particularly prevalent in the context of armed conflict, such as sexual exploitation, enslavement, and forced marriage; forced labor to support military operations; recruitment and exploitation of child soldiers; and removal of organs to treat injured fighters or finance operations.

Traffickers also target forcibly displaced populations. On migration routes, human traffickers deceive people into fraudulent travel arrangements and job opportunities. Migrants face unique danger as they go through holding points and informal settlements or accept unsafe employment opportunities. Refugee women and girls are at particular risk of sex trafficking and forced marriage.[11]

Figure 1. MAIN DETECTED TRANSREGIONAL TRAFFICKING FLOWS, 2014–2017

Thicker arrows → represent up to 95 percent of detected trafficking flows in destination countries. Thinner arrows → represent less than 5 percent of detected victims in destination countries.

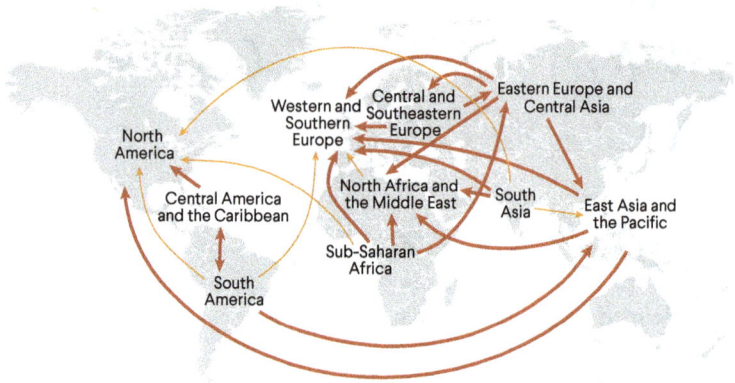

Note: Most trafficking flows are based on data from destination countries. The following flows are based on repatriation data from victims' countries of origin: from Central and Southeastern Europe and sub-Saharan Africa to Eastern Europe and Central Asia; from Eastern Europe and Central Asia and South America to East Asia and the Pacific.

Source: UN Office on Drugs and Crime, *Global Report on Trafficking in Persons 2018.*

SEX TRAFFICKING

Sex trafficking takes various forms during armed conflict, including sexual exploitation, sexual slavery, and forced marriage. It is perpetrated by a range of different actors, including armed and violent extremist groups, criminal networks, peacekeepers, representatives from nongovernmental and multilateral organizations, national militaries, and corrupt and complicit government officials. Sex trafficking is sometimes employed as a deliberate tactic by terrorist groups—including the Islamic State and Boko Haram—to attract, retain, mobilize, and reward male fighters by promising them sex slaves.[12] Although women and girls make up the vast majority of detected victims worldwide, sex trafficking is also committed against men and boys.

Figure 2. DETECTED VICTIMS OF TRAFFICKING IN PERSONS, 2016 (OR MOST RECENT)

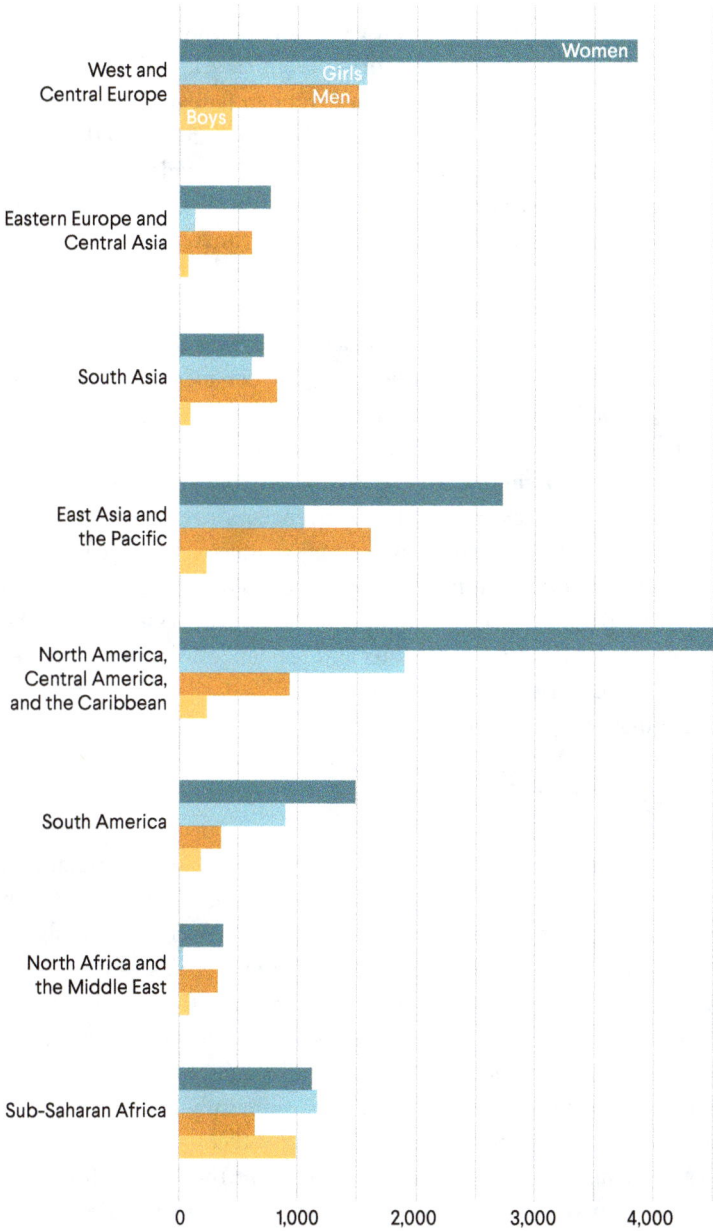

Source: UN Office on Drugs and Crime, *Global Report on Trafficking in Persons 2018*.

In areas where military personnel are deployed, rates of sexual exploitation increase.[13] During World War II, an estimated two hundred thousand "comfort women" were forced into prostitution in brothels serving the Japanese military. Many were Korean women who had been offered false promises of education, foreign travel, and high-paying jobs.[14] UN peacekeepers and personnel frequently sexually exploit and abuse the very citizens they are tasked with protecting. Two thousand allegations were lodged against UN missions worldwide from 2005 to 2016; in 2018, UN peacekeepers faced allegations of sexual exploitation or abuse in countries including the Central African Republic, Haiti, and South Sudan.[15]

The risks of sex trafficking are exacerbated by conflict-induced displacement. Across regions, displaced women and girls face particular vulnerabilities due to preexisting gender inequalities and the breakdown of legal and social protection systems. Interviews with Venezuelan women indicate that armed groups have demanded sex as payment for crossing the border into Colombia.[16] In China, female North Korean refugees are targeted by traffickers and forced into prostitution and marriages.[17] An overwhelming majority of female refugees and migrants interviewed in Libya by the United Nations in 2017 and 2018 reported either having been raped or having witnessed rape.[18] The difficulty of obtaining work permits and residence documents further places women at risk of sexual exploitation by landlords, employers, and criminal groups.[19]

LABOR TRAFFICKING

Throughout history, governments, armed groups, and criminal and extremist organizations in conflict settings have conducted human trafficking to generate revenue, support military operations, assist in illicit activities, and aid reconstruction. Armed groups often exploit members of ethnic minorities, people attempting to flee conflict, or abductees, forcing them to serve as porters, transport heavy military equipment, or assist in looting and pillaging.[20] In the Democratic Republic of Congo, armed groups forced internally displaced people to work in gold and mineral mines.[21] In postconflict situations, as countries start rebuilding societies and infrastructure, the demand for cheap labor may also lead to an increase in trafficking; in Iraq, Ukrainian construction workers were held against their will and subjected to forced labor at reconstruction sites.[22]

Refugees and migrants are at high risk of being trafficked into forced labor.[23] Their lack of legal status leaves refugees and migrants vulnerable to exploitation, with traffickers deliberately deceiving workers about their country of final destination and their living and working conditions.[24] In recent years, Rohingya Muslims fleeing genocide in Myanmar have migrated to Malaysia, where some have been forced into bonded labor on palm plantations and fishing boats in order to repay smugglers.[25]

USE OF CHILDREN BY ARMED GROUPS

The use and recruitment of children by armed and extremist groups nearly always constitutes human trafficking. In 2017, the United Nations verified more than 21,000 grave violations of children's rights during conflict, including the recruitment and use of child soldiers—an increase from 15,500 verified cases in 2016.[26] Yemen saw a fivefold increase in the number of children recruited between 2014 and 2015, and in the Central African Republic the number of recruited children quadrupled from 2016 to 2017.[27]

Some armed groups rely on children to sustain their military campaigns. Estimates suggest that in the early 2000s, 90 percent of forces in Central Africa's Lord's Resistance Army (LRA) were children, some as young as eight.[28] In addition, government forces around the world continue to recruit and use children to bolster their ranks: the United Nations investigated nearly 150 cases of children recruited by government forces in Myanmar in 2017.[29]

Extremist groups including al-Shabab, Boko Haram, the Islamic State, and the Taliban have abducted children to fuel their efforts.[30] In Liberia and Sierra Leone, government and rebel troops abducted girls and forced them to cook, launder clothes, and serve as porters.[31] Increasingly, terrorist groups are also using children to carry out suicide attacks: nearly 20 percent of suicide bombers used by Boko Haram in recent years were children or teenagers.[32] Similarly, the Islamic State has kidnapped and trained Yazidi boys to carry out suicide bombings.[33]

Children are especially vulnerable to trafficking by armed groups because of displacement, separation from their families, or inability to attend school.[34] Although recruitment of children usually involves coercion or abduction, some families and communities hand children over to armed groups out of a sense of obligation, particularly if the group is perceived as a security guarantor or if the group shares ethnic, religious, or geographic ties.[35] Children may also join armed groups to earn money when other survival options are elusive: in Sudan, children from the impoverished and battle-scarred region of Darfur were recruited to fight alongside Saudi-allied forces in Yemen with the lure of salaries that, while meager, nevertheless represented a lifeline for their families.[36]

The broad reach of the internet and social media and the ease of international travel also facilitate trafficking, including child trafficking, by armed groups. Extremists use social media to groom vulnerable teenagers and bait them into joining armed groups. The Islamic State is particularly savvy and sophisticated in its use of social media—for example, it launched a social media campaign to target Western women and girls from the United States and across Europe to help build the caliphate.[37]

ORGAN TRAFFICKING

Conflict also gives rise to organ trafficking, with traffickers taking advantage of weakened rule of law and the increased vulnerability of displaced populations to remove organs from people to generate revenue or treat injured fighters.[38] Victims of organ trafficking are recruited through deception, coercion, and exploitation of vulnerabilities, such as poverty; many are unaware of the nature of the procedure or the effect on their health.[39] In recent years, African migrants—many fleeing conflict—have been forced to sell their organs for passage into Europe.[40] Displaced Syrians have been subjected to organ trafficking: refugees have sold their organs in exchange for money and assistance with immigration authorities in Lebanon.[41] The Islamic State has used stolen organs to finance its war activities and to treat injured fighters, sanctioning the removal of organs from a living "apostate" captive to save a Muslim's life even if the captive will die.[42] The illicit organ trade is lucrative; demand is high and buyers may pay up to $80,000 to secure a kidney outside the formal transplant process.[43] Up to 10 percent of all transplants are thought to be conducted using illicitly acquired organs, and by some estimates, organ trafficking raises between $840 million and $1.7 billion annually in proceeds.[44] Terrorist groups, such as Jabhat Fateh al-Sham, have seized upon this opportunity to raise revenue.[45]

FORCED MARRIAGE

Conflict can exacerbate the risk of forced marriage, which has been reported in armed conflicts across regions including Africa, Asia, and the Middle East. Women and girls are the primary victims of this form of trafficking, often forced to tend to household duties while enduring physical and emotional violence.[46] Both the LRA and Sierra Leone's Revolutionary United Front abducted and coerced women and girls to become "bush wives," forcing them to marry combatants as well as to clean, cook, and sometimes participate in armed attacks.[47] Extremist groups also traffic women and girls for the purpose of forced marriage: the Islamic State recruited thousands of male affiliates by promising kidnapped women and girls as "wives."[48]

IMPLICATIONS
FOR U.S. INTERESTS

Human trafficking in conflict settings supports terrorist and armed groups, bankrolls criminal groups and transnational crime syndicates, supports abusive regimes, fosters instability, weakens governance, and impairs international cooperation, thereby undermining U.S. interests in global stability and security.

SUPPORTING TERRORIST AND ARMED GROUPS

Armed groups use trafficking to boost recruitment, generate revenue, expand military capabilities, and support operations, including by using victims as combatants, messengers, cooks, porters, and spies.[49] In recent years, some violent extremist groups—including the Islamic State and Boko Haram—have adopted the enslavement of populations as a policy rather than a covert practice, using human trafficking not only for forced labor and profit but also as a strategic tool to subjugate civilians.[50] The Islamic State's Research and Fatwa Department recently published explicit guidelines on how to treat female slaves—including rules on which women it is permissible to sell—and provided ideological justifications for human slavery, defending the practice of sex slaves with theological and historical references.[51] The Islamic State also systematically barters and sells women and girls as commodities through sales contracts notarized by Islamic State–run courts.[52] These crimes generate significant revenue: in 2013 alone, ransom payments extracted by the Islamic State amounted to between $35 and $45 million.[53]

In northern Nigeria and the Lake Chad region, Boko Haram similarly abducts women and girls to exchange prisoners, generate payments through ransom, or lure security forces to an ambush.[54] Some kidnapped women and girls are coerced into perpetrating suicide attacks:

one study found that over 50 percent of Boko Haram's suicide bombers were women.[55] Boko Haram has notoriously gone after schoolgirls as part of its campaign, kidnapping 276 female students from Chibok in Borno State in 2014 and generating an international outcry. Most of the captives were subjected to domestic servitude, forced labor, sexual slavery, forced marriage, and conversion. Boko Haram extracted approximately $3.7 million in ransom for the Chibok girls.[56]

In addition to generating profit, sex trafficking also advances armed groups' aims by decimating communities and denigrating the enemy. Yazidi leaders decreed that kidnapped Yazidi women would be welcomed back into the community, but left it up to families to decide whether to accept children whose fathers were Islamic State fighters—a decision that has forced many Yazidi women to choose between returning home or remaining with their children.[57] These enduring social and economic consequences weaken communities and reduce their resilience, thereby advancing the strategic aims of terrorist groups.[58]

BANKROLLING CRIMINAL ACTIVITY

Trafficking in persons is one of the most lucrative forms of organized crime and is generally thought to be a low-risk, high-profit enterprise for criminal organizations and transnational crime syndicates.[59] The steady demand for forced labor and prostitution allows traffickers to pass along to clients any extra costs they might incur, thereby protecting their financial gains.[60] Human trafficking also enables criminal groups to diversify their funding streams and criminal activities: in Mexico, large drug trafficking organizations have splintered into smaller groups that specialize in particular forms of crime, including human trafficking. These groups are flatter and more nimble, and they tend to resist pressure to limit violence.[61] Criminal organizations may also "multitask" by pairing human trafficking with other criminal activities—for example, using trafficking victims to transport drugs, which can generate large profits.[62]

Conflict provides criminal groups with an opportunity to profit from human trafficking. Nigeria's criminal networks benefit enormously from trafficking and have profited from conflict in Libya. Enhanced border security measures at the Lagos, Nigeria, airport could have cut down on trafficking were it not for the governance vacuum in Libya, which enables traffickers to transport victims overland through Libya.[63] In 2016, approximately eleven thousand Nigerian women arrived in Italy via Libya, 80 percent of whom were destined for sexual exploitation in Europe.[64]

An increase in poverty due to conflict compounds vulnerability to trafficking. Impoverished Iraqi refugees receive offers of up to $6,000 to sell their daughters to trafficking rings associated with criminal networks.[65] In Ukraine, Russia's annexation of Crimea and military involvement in eastern Ukraine has also led to an increase in human trafficking. Poverty, displacement, and restricted access to international aid has rendered local populations—particularly women—vulnerable to exploitation by criminal organizations.[66]

SUPPORTING ABUSIVE REGIMES

Some repressive governments traffic their citizens and compel them to labor in harsh conditions in order to bolster the economy, circumvent sanctions, or suppress dissent. During World War II, Nazi Germany's economy and war efforts relied on millions of forced laborers, including civilians from occupied Europe, prisoners of war, and concentration camp inmates.[67] More recently, international human rights groups have condemned the Eritrean mandatory service requirement, which conscripts all eighteen-year-olds into indefinite national service, including in the military, education, agriculture, and construction in foreign government–owned mineral mines.[68] Eritrean conscripts are poorly compensated and subjected to abusive conditions that are akin to forced labor, with women often singled out for particularly harsh punishment and sexual abuse.[69] Governments also rely on human trafficking and forced labor to circumvent sanctions: the North Korean government has sent nearly one hundred thousand laborers to work abroad, mainly in China and Russia, often in harsh conditions. The regime has thereby generated more than $500 million annually, helping it limit the effects of economic sanctions.[70] In addition, governments may use forced labor as a means to repress or discriminate against certain populations or as punishment for the expression of political views.[71] Approximately four million people were entrapped in state-imposed forced labor at any given point in 2016, many of whom were also victims of trafficking.[72] Such government-sponsored human rights abuses contribute to mass displacement and regional instability.

FOSTERING INSTABILITY

Human trafficking can destabilize communities, thereby exacerbating conflict and undermining development.[73] Fear of human trafficking drives displacement, which deprives communities of human potential and weakens essential support structures, thus fostering instability. In the Sinjar region of northern Iraq, threats of abduction by the Islamic State drove two hundred thousand Yazidis to flee from the Islamic State's rule in fifteen months.[74] Not all managed to escape; many were killed or enslaved.[75] And in Central America's Northern Triangle region—El Salvador, Guatemala, and Honduras—many women report that increasing levels of gang violence, which includes human trafficking, was a major factor in their decision to migrate.[76]

The strategic and financial benefits of human trafficking also enable armed and extremist groups to expand their power and capabilities, thereby prolonging conflict.[77] The human costs that trafficking exacts on communities are detrimental and long lasting: the devastating effects of this crime and the associated stigma—particularly in instances of sexual exploitation and children being used by armed groups—unravels kinship networks and marginalizes survivors, resulting in isolation. For women and girls, it can mean a loss of employment and marriage prospects and ostracism for children born of rape, thereby creating a cycle of poverty that is difficult to break.[78] In postconflict situations, the failure to address human trafficking can impede the chances of rebuilding societies and creating long-term stability.[79]

Human trafficking can also contribute to financial instability, particularly where armed groups and warlords take advantage of institutional instability to further their profits from trafficking.[80] Despite anti–money laundering programs, human traffickers continue to use financial services to manage and launder money. When financial institutions fail to identify bad actors exploiting their services, they risk not only financial consequences such as steep fines, remediation costs, and declines in corporate share values, but also reputational harm.[81] Failure of financial institutions to detect and prevent illicit behavior can lead people to believe that banks and regulators are neither credible nor properly functioning, thereby further destabilizing societies.

WEAKENING GOVERNANCE

The real and perceived corruption that fuels human trafficking—as well as the failure of governments to address it—erodes faith in public institutions. Government officials are sometimes complicit in human trafficking: they help traffickers recruit, transport, and exploit victims, and corrupt criminal justice authorities impede prosecutions or fail to provide victims with adequate protection.[82] Often traffickers will maintain control over their victims in destination countries by threatening that if they manage to escape, officials will return them to their captors.[83] The vast majority of trafficking cases are not reported, investigated, or prosecuted, further reinforcing public distrust in government. Transnational criminal groups also threaten family members of trafficking victims, including through the use of retaliation, which contributes to underreporting.

UNDERMINING INTERNATIONAL COOPERATION

Peacekeeping missions have contributed to an increase in human trafficking, including in the Balkans, Haiti, and Sierra Leone. Between 2001 and 2011, the presence of peacekeeping forces was positively correlated with forced prostitution.[84] In recent years, UN peacekeepers were accused of more than one hundred cases of sexual exploitation in the Central African Republic, and in Haiti allegations included reports of peacekeepers luring children with candy and money and then sexually abusing them.[85]

Similarly, an increased presence of military personnel can fuel the demand for sexually exploitative services.[86] In South Korea between the 1960s and 1980s, South Korean women were trafficked to brothels visited frequently by U.S. military personnel, tricked by job-placement agencies and held in debt to pimps who managed a network of prostitution camps.[87] The trafficking of women around U.S. bases in South Korea has remained a problem; in more recent years, foreign women—including from China, the Philippines, and Russia—are increasingly replacing South Korean women as victims of sex trafficking and prostitution.[88] Commercial sex zones have emerged close to several U.S.

military bases around the world, from Fort Bragg in North Carolina to Baumholder in Germany.[89] Following the 1999 North Atlantic Treaty Organization (NATO) intervention in Kosovo, the influx of military personnel from NATO countries transformed a small-scale market for prostitution that focused on catering to UN peacekeepers deployed in the early 1990s into a large-scale sex trafficking industry led by organized criminal groups.[90] In addition, police and military personnel in countries around the world have been complicit in trafficking: in one example over the last decade, local military officials at security checkpoints in Sudan and Egypt returned victims to traffickers who had kidnapped and trafficked displaced Eritreans.[91]

The U.S. government has also been implicated in labor trafficking in conflict areas. In 2006, U.S. government inspectors uncovered abuses by U.S. Department of Defense (DOD) contractors who were hiring workers from third-party countries to work on U.S. bases in Iraq. Recruiters and intermediaries in the laborers' countries of origin employed deceptive hiring practices and charged laborers excessive fees, and victims then lived and worked under substandard conditions on U.S. bases, with DOD contractors withholding passports to prevent them from leaving the country.[92]

Human trafficking committed or permitted by peacekeepers and security forces undermines the integrity of international institutions that promote peace and stability, hinders their ability to carry out critical missions, and runs counter to U.S. security interests. Involvement of peacekeepers in human trafficking damages public perceptions of the United Nations. Opponents of multilateralism in the United States point to abuses by UN peacekeepers as justification for reducing U.S. investment in international institutions, even though these institutions are critical to broader global stability.

Human trafficking is also an affront to core U.S. values, including the right to freedom and dignity and a commitment to justice and the rule of law. Perpetrating sex and labor trafficking and failing to hold traffickers accountable undermines the United States' standing on other human rights issues and diminishes U.S. influence in security efforts.

CONSIDERATIONS FOR U.S. POLICY

Combating trafficking is deeply tied to U.S. national security interests, including countering terrorism and organized crime, conflict prevention and stabilization, and multilateral cooperation. Ignoring its spread undermines efforts to advance a more peaceful and secure world. Yet human trafficking is rarely considered a budgetary or strategic priority. The Trump administration should prioritize anti-trafficking measures and mainstream this issue in existing conflict prevention, anti-crime, counterterrorism, and stabilization efforts by increasing investment, reporting, and prosecution.

CURRENT U.S. AND GLOBAL POLICY

In the United States, efforts to address human trafficking increased after the U.S. Congress passed the Trafficking Victims Protection Act of 2000. Officials in the three most recent presidential administrations have taken steps to address the ways in which human trafficking undermines U.S. security interests. The George W. Bush administration established the President's Interagency Task Force to Monitor and Combat Trafficking in Persons in 2002; the Barack Obama administration issued a National Intelligence Estimate on global human trafficking in 2016; and in 2017, the Trump administration issued an executive order directing law enforcement agencies to enhance cooperation with foreign counterparts to identify, interdict, disrupt, and dismantle transnational criminal organizations that conduct trafficking.[93] Numerous agencies across the U.S. government have created programs, offices, and initiatives focused on combating human trafficking internationally. These initiatives, which include the U.S. Department of State's annual Trafficking in Persons (TIP) reports, the Counter–Trafficking in Persons Policy of the U.S. Agency for International Development (USAID), and U.S. investment in the Global Fund to End Modern Slavery, show a long-standing bipartisan commitment.

Congress has demonstrated continued commitment to combating human trafficking. In January 2019, it reauthorized the seminal Trafficking Victims Protection Act with improved reporting and tighter criteria for determining whether countries meet the minimum standards for eliminating human trafficking and thus are eligible to receive foreign assistance. In recent years, Congress enacted a series of supporting laws, including the Abolish Human Trafficking Act, to provide greater assistance to victims, and the Allow States and Victims to Fight Online Sex Trafficking Act, to hold websites that host sex-trafficking ads accountable. Congress has also passed legislation to address specific forms of trafficking in conflict situations, including the Child Soldiers Prevention Act of 2008.

The United States also has numerous financial mechanisms that could be more consistently used to address trafficking in conflict settings. The Global Magnitsky Act, enacted in 2016, allows the president to freeze the assets of individuals who commit gross violations of human rights. A 2017 executive order broadened the mandate of the act to cover any "serious human rights abuse," thereby lowering the evidentiary threshold for inclusion. The Leahy Law, a provision in the Foreign Assistance and National Defense Authorization Acts, was enacted to cut U.S. assistance from partner security force units found to have committed "gross violations of human rights." The Department of the Treasury has created several offices that address trafficking through financial regulations: the Financial Crimes Enforcement Network advises financial institutions on how to detect activity related to human trafficking, the Office of Foreign

Assets Control administers sanctions against groups associated with the use of child soldiers, and the Office of Terrorism and Financial Intelligence tracks and combats terrorist activity.

Notwithstanding these steps, significant gaps remain in translating the U.S. government's rhetoric into consistent action, including in areas affected by conflict or terrorism. Few of these programs and policies have addressed the intersection of trafficking and national security or sufficiently addressed the compounding effect of conflict and migration on trafficking patterns. For example, the Department of Homeland Security's Blue Campaign, which educates the public and law enforcement about human trafficking, is chronically understaffed, while USAID's 2012 Counter–Trafficking in Persons Policy has not been updated to reflect recent trends surrounding displacement and migration. In 2018, the Trump administration announced it would not issue presidential waivers to countries ranked Tier 3 in the State Department's Trafficking in Persons report, thereby prohibiting non-humanitarian, non-trade aid to nearly twenty countries that are neither complying with minimum standards in preventing trafficking nor making significant efforts to do so. However, nongovernmental organizations allege that giving out fewer aid waivers results in more closures of programs that directly assist people in need, from addressing the current Ebola crisis in Congo to demining former war zones, and even to combating human trafficking.[94] Meanwhile, the Trump administration continues to issue national security waivers to five of eight countries identified by the State Department as using child soldiers, a practice carried on from the Obama administration.

The U.S. government does not invest much in using national security and intelligence tools to identify and disrupt human trafficking routes. The broader national security community does not communicate enough with officials focused on human rights and conflict prevention, resulting in missed opportunities to better leverage U.S. legal authorities, tools, and capacities to prevent human trafficking. U.S. human rights offices, such as those focused on human trafficking and those addressing conflict-related sexual violence, also do not coordinate enough. And despite the proliferation of resolutions, protocols, laws, and action plans focused on combating trafficking, it continues to be treated as a human rights issue that is ancillary to broader foreign policy concerns, including conflict prevention and counterterrorism.

Beyond the United States, in recent decades nations have created a comprehensive legal framework to prevent and outlaw human trafficking, including through the 2000 Protocol to Prevent, Suppress and Punish the Trafficking in Persons, Especially Women and Children, which has 117 signatories. This protocol supplemented the UN Convention Against Transnational Organized Crime, the first global legally binding instrument that includes a consensus on the definition of trafficking in persons. Today, almost every country has legislation in place that criminalizes human trafficking, and the number of convictions is increasing.[95]

Governments have also collaborated to bring greater attention to the issue of human trafficking and increase cross-border cooperation, including through the 2017 Call to Action to End Forced Labor, Modern Slavery and Human Trafficking and the Alliance 8.7 initiative—a global partnership dedicated to eradicating forced labor, modern slavery, human trafficking, and child labor (target 8.7 of the Sustainable Development Goals, or SDGs). The SDGs include three targets related to trafficking, with specific mention of eliminating sex trafficking of women and girls; forced labor, modern slavery, and child labor, including the use of child soldiers; and the exploitation and trafficking of children.[96] The Financial Action Task Force—established by a group of thirty-two nations to set global standards for combating threats to the international financial system—in 2011 published a comprehensive report analyzing financial flows from human trafficking, and a follow-up report in 2018 contained best practices and recommendations for member countries.[97] Overall, though, coordination between governments on anti-trafficking measures remains limited, with donor dialogues few and far between.

The UN Security Council and the broader UN system have also begun to recognize the security implications of human trafficking and its links with conflict, instability, and terrorism. For the first time in its history, the UN Security Council adopted a presidential statement in 2015 noting that trafficking in persons can exacerbate conflict and foster insecurity. In 2016, the Security Council adopted Resolution 2331, the first to recognize human trafficking as a tactic of terrorism that undermines broader conflict prevention and peacebuilding efforts. The resolution further noted that extremist and terrorist groups use sexual violence—including sexual slavery—as a tactic of terror. In 2017, the UN secretary-general called on the Security Council to include human trafficking criteria when adopting sanctions regimes in situations of armed conflict; in 2018, the Security Council sanctioned six individuals involved in the trafficking of migrants in Libya.[98]

The private sector is also taking steps to address human trafficking and conflict in its internal practices and supply chains by training employees and investing in anti-trafficking initiatives. Hotel chains Hilton and Marriott have partnered with nongovernmental organizations to train survivors of sex trafficking in the hospitality industry and help them secure long-term employment.[99] And JPMorgan worked with the Department of Homeland Security to develop technological tools to identify financial transaction patterns that were red flags for human trafficking, even in cases of low dollar transactions.[100]

Financial tracking, technological innovation, awareness programs, and public-private partnerships that focus broadly on combating trafficking and exploitation can be tailored to address trafficking exacerbated by conflict. Some states and nations are developing legislation to enforce corporate responsibility, such as the 2010 California Transparency in Supply Chains Act and the 2015 UK Modern Slavery Act, which require companies to disclose their efforts to eradicate human trafficking from their direct supply chains.[101] These requirements are particularly critical for businesses with supply chains in conflict-affected areas and in countries with high refugee populations.

RECOMMENDATIONS FOR THE UNITED STATES

U.S. security efforts that fail to account for the prospect of trafficking of vulnerable populations risk creating a situation in which traffickers can thrive, thereby threatening global stability and bolstering malicious actors, including terrorist groups, transnational crime networks, and repressive regimes. As part of the Trump administration's commitment to advancing U.S. security interests, the U.S. government should increase attention and resources to combating human trafficking.

Critics may question the allocation of attention and resources to the issue of trafficking, which has been seen as a concern primarily of human rights activists, not of the national security community. However, a growing body of research and evidence suggests that human trafficking fuels many of the paramount security challenges facing the United States, from the rise of extremism to continued destabilization in Afghanistan and Iraq. As security threats converge, human trafficking becomes a threat multiplier, financing other criminal activities and fomenting greater insecurity. Failing to identify and combat trafficking creates secondary and tertiary effects that undermine U.S. national security interests by allowing extremist groups to flourish, driving migrant flows, and reducing trust and cooperation among global partners.

To strengthen U.S. efforts to prevent trafficking and promote security, the White House—together with the intelligence community, the Departments of Defense, Justice, State, and the Treasury, and USAID—should work to disrupt and dismantle the criminal networks and terrorist groups that exploit conflict-related human trafficking, while prioritizing the prevention, prosecution, and protection from human trafficking in conflict contexts.

Disrupt and Dismantle Criminal Networks and Terrorist Groups

The Departments of State and the Treasury should use sanctions to freeze assets of human traffickers. The Treasury should issue new authorities to authorize and encourage the use of targeted sanctions to block assets raised through human trafficking. In the absence of new legislation, the Treasury should use existing authorities under the Global Magnitsky Act or the executive order Blocking Property of Transnational Criminal Organizations to address human trafficking crimes globally. In parallel, the U.S. government should encourage the UN Security Council to pass a resolution permitting the sanctions designation of human traffickers around the world. The U.S. government should also encourage countries to bring individuals and evidence forward to the Security Council to support trafficking-related designations.

The Department of the Treasury should urge other governments to adopt legislation to encourage data sharing related to suspicious financial activity. Section 314(a) of the USA Patriot Act and the resulting Financial Crimes Enforcement Network required the Treasury to adopt regulations that would encourage information sharing between regulatory and law enforcement actors and banks and other financial institutions in order to identify suspicious financial activity related to terrorist acts or money laundering activities—both of which could include human trafficking in conflict.[102] By offering protections from liability, Section 314(b) of the same act encourages financial institutions to share information with one another to better identify money laundering or terrorist activities. Enacting similar legislation throughout Europe and around the world would create a legal and regulatory framework to enable a greater number of banks to share data on transactions related to terrorism or money laundering—including human trafficking. Increased data sharing and greater collaboration across investigative networks would improve government efforts to investigate, disrupt, and dismantle human trafficking syndicates.

The Departments of Justice and the Treasury should report the number of cases they investigate and prosecute related to human trafficking in conflict or terrorist financing. The Department of the Treasury should work with other banking agencies to identify and draw on successful strategies to use anti–money laundering approaches to address human trafficking in conflict, including by closing policy or regulatory gaps and providing employee training. Risk assessments of illicit activities in the United States should include attention to human trafficking. The U.S. government should fund research on how human traffickers use virtual currency in conflict-affected contexts.

The U.S. government should strengthen the regulatory system to address money laundering in the virtual world. The internet has accelerated illicit trade and is dominated by a handful of companies. Although these companies are legitimate, they facilitate illegal transactions. Online markets are owned by private companies, so these spaces need to be regulated both by the companies themselves and by the U.S. government. The Departments of State and the Treasury should further encourage Group of Seven and Group of Twenty countries to develop a shared regulatory system to stop illicit trade that occurs in cyberspace.

The U.S. government should encourage greater analysis of financial flows associated with human trafficking in conflict and with human trafficking that finances terrorism. The Departments of State and the Treasury should encourage the Egmont Group of Financial Intelligence Units and the Financial Action Task Force to use and keep up to date human trafficking–relevant typologies, case studies, and red flag indicators. The U.S. government should ensure that its own financial intelligence units maintain expertise on human trafficking and encourage the same of other governments.

The U.S. intelligence and law enforcement communities should increase their monitoring of human trafficking connected to armed conflict and terrorism. From the Central Intelligence Agency to the Defense Intelligence Agency, the intelligence community should better track the exploitation of migrant and smuggling routes by criminal networks and terrorist groups, including by collecting information on human trafficking where the U.S. government already tracks drugs and arms trafficking. The Office of the Director of National Intelligence should elevate human trafficking to a higher priority in the National Intelligence Priorities Framework.

The U.S. Congress should require companies established in the United States to disclose their beneficial owners to the Financial Crimes

Enforcement Network when they incorporate and to continuously update this information. Currently, the United States is one of the most financially secretive countries in the world.[103] Criminals, terrorists, and traffickers have taken advantage of gaps in U.S. legislation to open anonymous shell corporations to access the U.S. banking system, enabling terrorist financing, money laundering by criminal organizations, and countries evading sanctions. Passing legislation would help law enforcement combat terrorism, criminal activity, and other threats—including human trafficking.

Improve Prevention

U.S. government policies on human trafficking should include a stronger focus on conflict, and policies on conflict-related issues should include a stronger focus on human trafficking. USAID should update its Counter–Trafficking in Persons Policy every five years; the 2012 policy should be revised with greater attention to recent migration trends and the incidence of human trafficking in conflict, as well as human trafficking and terrorist financing. Agency implementation plans for the 2019 Women, Peace, and Security Strategy should expand on opportunities for U.S. staff focused on gender and trafficking issues to better collaborate in addressing conflict-related human trafficking of women and girls.

The Defense and State Departments should include training to identify and prevent human trafficking in all U.S. security cooperation efforts. This training requirement would build on the 2017 National Defense Authorization Act, which required security cooperation efforts to be accompanied by training on human rights. More courses offered by the U.S. Defense Institute of International Legal Studies should include information on how partner security forces can combat trafficking in persons.

The Departments of Labor and State should urge corporate due diligence to protect against industry involvement in human trafficking in conflict. In line with the U.S. government's 2016 National Action Plan on Responsible Business Conduct, the Departments of Labor and State should ensure a focus on conflict-affected areas in their research on trafficking and forced-labor prevention in federal and corporate supply chains. The U.S. government should continue to work with U.S. companies and civil society to develop conflict-free supply chains, such as by sourcing certified minerals from the African Great Lakes region.

The State Department should incentivize private-sector efforts to create promising technologies to prevent human trafficking in conflict contexts. The U.S. government should promote efforts by the information and communications technology sector to combat human trafficking, potentially through the use of social media and other communications tools. The United States should also support Tech Against Trafficking and other coalitions of global technology companies, civil society organizations, and international institutions to include a focus on conflict-related human trafficking.

The State Department and USAID should invest in research and analysis on the relationship between human trafficking, conflict, and terrorism. The State Department's and USAID's conflict monitoring tools should include analyses of the relationship between human trafficking and broader conflict dynamics, including postconflict economies. These analyses should also identify how the U.S. government can disincentivize human trafficking by armed or terrorist groups, including through peacebuilding, sanctions, and broader accountability efforts.

The U.S. Congress should pass legislation, modeled on California's approach, requiring that companies with annual global receipts exceeding $100 million publicly disclose their efforts to address forced labor, slavery, and human trafficking in their supply chains. Congress could, for example, reintroduce and pass the Business Supply Chain Transparency on Trafficking and Slavery Act of 2018, specifying the responsibility of companies to investigate supply chain practices in conflict-affected regions.

The U.S. Congress should pass legislation that requires social media companies to monitor their platforms for suspicious online activity. In line with the 2018 Allow States and Victims to Fight Online Sex Trafficking Act, social media companies should be required to implement anti–human trafficking compliance programs.

Increase Prosecution

The U.S. government should support accountability for trafficking-related crimes. Today, only a small number of trafficking cases leads to conviction—a gap that widens in conflict-affected areas. As the U.S. government invests in rule-of-law initiatives across law enforcement, justice, and social service providers in conflict-affected contexts, it should provide targeted support for coordinated anti-trafficking efforts. To fight corruption related to human trafficking, such efforts should include a focus on investigating and prosecuting corrupt public officials profiting from such crimes. The U.S. government should also train border officials along migration and smuggling routes from conflict-affected areas to identify and support trafficking victims.

The U.S. government should pursue charges against Islamic State affiliates for sexual slavery and other forms of human trafficking. This would ensure accountability for these crimes while providing a direct response to the Islamic State's explicit strategy of profiting from slavery and trafficking. The U.S. government should work with partner nations, including those in the Global Coalition to Defeat ISIS, to provide technical assistance to the Iraqi government to find and free the estimated three thousand Yazidi women and girls abducted and enslaved by the Islamic State.

The State Department and the U.S. Mission to the United Nations should pressure the UN secretary-general to remove the heads of peacekeeping missions who fail to address sexual exploitation and abuse by UN peacekeepers and officials in conflict areas. Recognizing that such exploitation can create conditions permissive to sex trafficking, the U.S. government should encourage the United Nations to prioritize accountability as well as redress for victims.

The Defense and State Departments should use all available tools to encourage partner militaries to end the use of child soldiers. The Child Soldiers Prevention Act is intended to prohibit countries that use child soldiers from receiving U.S. military assistance and weapons. The Trump administration should take this commitment seriously, rather than routinely issuing full waivers of these sanctions to allow continued assistance. Further, the U.S. Congress should request greater transparency in the listing of offending countries to reconcile discrepancies between State Department listings and verifiable documentation of child soldier use, and should enact a procedure that allows it to disapprove of a waiver by joint resolution.

Strengthen Protection

The U.S. government should encourage peacekeeping missions to better protect civilians from trafficking in conflict. The State Department and the U.S. Mission to the United Nations should consistently advocate for peacekeeping mission mandates to take concrete steps to prevent human trafficking. The Defense and State Departments should lead an effort to improve peacekeepers' preparedness to identify and protect civilians from trafficking, including through mandatory pre-deployment training. Furthermore, the U.S. government should encourage the United Nations to adopt protocols that facilitate UN peacekeeping missions to share information on human trafficking threats with relevant financial and law enforcement organizations, like the Egmont Group and the International Criminal Police Organization (Interpol).

The State Department and USAID should encourage the humanitarian community to better protect those vulnerable to human trafficking in conflict. The humanitarian cluster system, which improves the coordination of assistance delivered by humanitarian organizations, only recently designated human trafficking as a protection priority. The State Department and USAID should encourage the UN agencies and humanitarian organizations, including the Office of the UN High Commissioner for Refugees (UNHCR)—the cluster protection lead—to incorporate antislavery and anti-trafficking efforts into their humanitarian activities in conflict-affected areas and to increase their consultations with and support for anti-trafficking partners. In recognition of the risks posed by conflict-related emergencies to those vulnerable to human trafficking, the U.S. government should encourage humanitarian actors to include risk analysis of human trafficking at the outset of, and throughout, any humanitarian response effort.

The State Department and USAID should invest at least $150 million per year in comprehensive services for survivors of human trafficking in conflict. These services should include medical and psychosocial care and livelihood assistance, as well as broader support for family tracing and reunification. The State Department and USAID should further encourage the various global funds focused on human trafficking to explicitly address the needs of victims of human trafficking in conflict.

The State Department and USAID should invest in multilateral programs for the disarmament, demobilization, and reintegration (DDR) of former child soldiers. There is urgent need for greater access to DDR programs to prevent re-recruitment and long-term trauma and to help ensure that child survivors of trafficking in conflict receive adequate resources for rehabilitation, as well as educational and vocational opportunities.

The State Department should encourage public-private partnerships that provide vocational training to survivors of conflict-related trafficking. Successful examples of corporate initiatives providing employment assistance for victims of sex trafficking or refugee populations can be expanded to target populations trafficked as a result of conflict.

Since entering office, the Trump administration has made immigration policy a priority. Beginning in 2017, Trump has issued numerous executive orders to tighten eligibility for legal immigration, increase vetting of visa applicants, eliminate protections for noncitizens, and expand security enforcement at the southern border. The thirty-thousand-refugee admission cap in 2019 is the lowest since the Refugee Act of 1980 created the modern refugee resettlement program. Collectively, these policies have drastically reduced the avenues for legal immigration and raised the costs for individuals and families seeking to resettle in the United States. By making the journey riskier, they contribute to migrants' vulnerability to human trafficking and discourage trafficking survivors from seeking help.

In addition, Trump has made stemming the flow of migrants from Central American countries a major goal for his administration. In 2018, then Attorney General Jeff Sessions ruled that domestic and gang violence are not grounds for asylum, in an attempt to reduce the number of asylum seekers. In May 2018, the Trump administration implemented its so-called zero-tolerance policy, under which the U.S. Department of Justice can prosecute all adults apprehended crossing the border anywhere other than at a port of entry. There has been no exception for asylum seekers or those with minor children. Despite these policies, the number of Central Americans crossing the southwest border continues to increase. In May 2019 alone, 144,000 migrants and asylum seekers were taken into custody at the southern border—a 32 percent increase from the month before. In June 2019, the Trump administration announced that it would reduce aid to El Salvador, Guatemala, and Honduras and that future funding to the region would be contingent upon these governments' efforts to reduce migrant outflows. However, a reduction in U.S. foreign assistance is likely to increase the number of migrants and asylum seekers, as less funding will go toward addressing the root causes of migration, such as corruption, poverty, and violence.

Though migration flows can exacerbate human trafficking, there is little evidence that extremist fighters have used smuggling routes to enter Europe or the United States. The vast majority of terrorist attacks perpetrated in the United States and Europe are committed by citizens.[104] The U.S. vetting system permitted entry of one radicalized extremist per twenty-nine million visa approvals.[105] By another count, as of 2015, only three of the more than 850,000 refugees admitted to the United States since 2001 had been convicted of planning terrorist attacks on targets outside the United States; none of the attacks was executed successfully.[106]

The U.S. government should ensure that its policies on migration and asylum disincentivize trafficking and support survivors. Stringent border controls can increase vulnerability to trafficking; the U.S. government should evaluate whether its current and proposed border policies contribute to an increase in human trafficking. The Trump administration should instruct the Department of Homeland Security to revert to the previous process for issuing T nonimmigrant status (or T visas, which provide legal status to immigrant victims of human trafficking who are willing to assist law enforcement in the investigation and prosecution of their traffickers). In that process, the U.S. Citizenship and Immigration Services handled applications internally and were not required to refer information about denied visa applications to other agencies. Congress should also conduct oversight hearings on the U.S. attorney general's ruling in Matter of A-B-, which blocks a pathway to safety for domestic violence victims claiming asylum. The Department of Homeland Security should increase investment in the Blue Campaign, which is currently underfunded and understaffed.

The U.S. government should support Northern Triangle countries in preventing and addressing gender-based violence, including that perpetrated by violent gangs. This investment will not only protect and empower women and girls but will also help the administration address the drivers of irregular migration from these countries to the United States, and thereby reduce it. Passing the Central American Women and Children Protection Act of 2019 would be a starting point.

The United States should ensure stronger compliance with its government-wide zero-tolerance policy on human trafficking, including by personnel and contractors and throughout its procurement systems. There are documented gaps in the Defense Department's response, for example; to address these, the department should create a new office with Senate-confirmed leadership to oversee efforts to combat human trafficking—including scenario-based and mission-specific training and awareness campaigns, vendor vetting, and support for investigations.[107] The department should further assess opportunities for the U.S. Cyber Command to address online aspects of human trafficking, building on previous efforts of the Defense Advanced Research Projects Agency.[108] This office would liaise across the department, with contractors, international and regional organizations including the United Nations and North Atlantic Treaty Organization, and partner militaries.

The U.S. government should improve the accuracy of its estimate of the number of human trafficking victims in the United States. Many cases of human trafficking go unreported and are therefore unaccounted for in national statistics. A new UN methodology employs statistical techniques to estimate a more accurate victim count, which would allow the U.S. government to develop more targeted policy interventions to detect and provide support services to previously hidden victims of trafficking.[109]

CONCLUSION

The serious and far-reaching security implications of human trafficking in conflict and terrorism-affected areas demonstrate why the United States should elevate this issue on the national security agenda. To advance stability, the U.S. government should include anti-trafficking measures in conflict prevention, antiterrorism, anti-crime, and peace-building efforts, and prioritize the identification and disruption of armed and extremist groups and criminal organizations that perpetrate human trafficking.

APPENDIX
Case Studies

The relationship between trafficking in persons, conflict, corruption, organized crime, and terrorism demonstrates why policymakers need to address trafficking as a security issue. In Iraq, human trafficking has been used by the Islamic State to terrorize communities and recruit fighters, thereby undermining efforts to promote stability and establish civilians' trust in government. In Libya, trafficking of African migrants in conflict zones and fragile environments has destabilized existing power-sharing networks. In Myanmar, persecuted minorities—including the Muslim Rohingya—have been trafficked and exploited by transnational criminal groups that profit from the dire humanitarian situation. And in Central America's Northern Triangle, migrants journeying north are exploited ruthlessly by criminals, affirming the need for functional and secure immigration systems.

IRAQ

In Iraq, human trafficking has undermined efforts to promote stability and has been used as a tactic by the Islamic State to spread terror among civilian populations and recruit fighters. Weak rule of law, large-scale displacement, and conflict have exposed civilians in Iraq and Iraqi Kurdistan to increased risk of trafficking, including forced labor, child soldiering, sex trafficking, and forced marriages. Reconstruction projects have created a demand for foreign labor, and migrant workers from Asia and East Africa who were originally recruited for work in other countries in the region have been forced, coerced, or deceived into working in Iraq and Iraqi Kurdistan. They are subjected to forced labor as construction workers, security guards, domestic workers, and cleaners.[110]

The Islamic State has used trafficking to spread terror among civilians, recruit fighters, and bolster its military capacity. In 2014, the Islamic State launched an assault on Yazidi communities in the Mount Sinjar region of Iraqi Kurdistan, massacring Yazidi men and boys of fighting age and abducting over 6,300 Yazidis, including more than 3,500 women.[111] The Islamic State sought to create the "next generation of jihadists" through forced insemination and pregnancies.[112] Boys between the ages of eight and seventeen were referred to as the "Cubs of the Caliphate," and they were indoctrinated and trained to serve in conflict and support roles, including as bomb makers, executioners, human shields, informants, and suicide bombers.[113] After the Islamic State's defeat, many of these boys were placed in detention centers, or returned to their families without receiving the care and support that trafficking victims require.

Although the governments of Iraq and Iraqi Kurdistan have taken steps to address and prevent human trafficking, they could do considerably more. Continued insecurity, limited budgets, and massive reconstruction efforts limit both governments' ability to allocate resources toward preventing trafficking, holding perpetrators accountable, and assisting victims. Government efforts to identify victims are inadequate, and victims are vulnerable to arrest and deportation for unlawful acts committed as a direct result of being subject to human trafficking. Despite the security implications of labor trafficking in Iraq and Iraqi Kurdistan, their anti-trafficking laws fail to criminalize all forms of labor and sex trafficking, and penalties for labor trafficking are weak.[114] In Iraqi Kurdistan, some of the few trafficking cases taken to court have been tried under Iraq's Penal Code or Anti-Prostitution Act, which led to the prosecution of the victim.[115] Law enforcement and judicial officials tasked with handling trafficking cases lack the necessary specialized training to do so. Although the Iraqi government established its first shelter for victims of trafficking in 2018, it is rarely used and lacks reintegration and repatriation programs. In Iraqi Kurdistan, more shelters are needed and should be sufficiently resourced; women require a court order to be allowed protection at the existing government shelters for women, even though some women prefer not to involve courts.[116] The failure of the governments in Iraq and Iraqi Kurdistan to address human trafficking undermines their ability to build trust among civilians and promote stability.

In Libya, the lack of a stable government, economic opportunities, and security—combined with a breakdown of the rule of law and the rise of militias fighting for control and power—has created a fertile ground for traffickers. Armed militias have used trafficking to increase their resources and expand their political power.[117] Trafficking in Libya has also exacerbated the risk of conflict, as it has upended existing power-sharing networks and provided marginalized groups who lost out during the 2011 revolution the opportunity to gain more power.[118]

In recent years, tens of thousands of African migrants and refugees have traveled the Mediterranean route to Italy, passing through Libya. Traffickers have seized on the increased flow of vulnerable migrants, with some even impersonating UNHCR staff, wearing clothing with logos that resemble UNHCR's.[119] Men and boys report high levels of sexual violence and trafficking perpetrated against them at checkpoints, in clandestine prisons, and in Libyan detention centers. Women and girls report sexual abuse during their journey through Libya and in migrant detention centers, perpetrated by smugglers, traffickers, members of armed groups, and government officials.[120]

Along migration routes, armed groups impose "passage taxes" and offer protection to smugglers' convoys in exchange for payment—a scheme that has generated significant profit.[121] Some female migrants are asked to pay a higher fee to smugglers or are expected to raise money along their travels: Nigerian women report that smugglers sold them to brothel owners who then forced them to work as prostitutes until they were able to pay double the amount it had cost to buy them.[122] Others report being punished with sexual abuse and starvation if they refused to work and being attacked during "night parties."[123] Some of the victims have been forcibly returned to their home countries by the Libyan coast guard, operating under EU-endorsed policies.[124]

Armed groups have used migrants and refugees for debt bondage, forced labor, and sexual exploitation.[125] Libyan militias have taken migrants from Chad, Niger, and Nigeria into their ranks, using them for labor and noncombat roles.[126] Some migrants have been locked up in detention centers controlled by local militias and forced to carry and stockpile weapons, which helps fuel armed conflict in these areas.[127] Recently, militias have started to raid migrant houses and intercept migrant boats in an effort to portray themselves as partners of the European Union in tackling illegal migration; this allows them to receive EU funding. Simultaneously, militias continue to profit from the migrant trade, including by smuggling migrants and providing protection to other smugglers.[128] The financial flows raised from trafficking have allowed these groups to build up their militias, resulting in a power struggle between competing groups.[129]

Extremist groups, including the Islamic State, have also exploited the large exodus of African migrants traveling through Libya toward Europe. According to witnesses, Islamic State fighters abducted hundreds of refugees in ambushes in Libya between 2015 and 2016, some of whom they sold as sex slaves to attract and reward fighters in Libya.[130] The group has also taken advantage of the large refugee and migrant flows for financial gains, taxing smugglers in exchange for passage and using already established smuggling routes to recruit new fighters.[131] Despite these trends, Libya has not criminalized labor trafficking and only recently criminalized some forms of sex trafficking—though, contrary to international law, Libya's definition of sex trafficking requires transnational movement and does not cover acts that were induced through fraudulent or coercive means, or acts involving adult male victims.[132]

MYANMAR

Trafficking in Myanmar occurs through the exploitation of the minority Muslim Rohingya displaced population, the recruitment and use of child soldiers, and forced labor in the armed forces. Public officials and ethnic minority insurgencies benefit directly from trafficking in persons, while the civilian government remains complicit, stonewalling efforts that could ameliorate the situation. In its 2019 TIP report, the U.S. State Department kept Myanmar at the lowest-ranking level for the second year in a row, citing the government's failure to fully comply with the minimum standards to eliminate trafficking, punctuated by zero enforcement of its 2005 Anti–Trafficking in Persons Law.[133]

Persecution of the Rohingya by the Myanmar government, military, and local vigilante groups in western Myanmar has caused a dire humanitarian situation, forcing an exodus of hundreds of thousands of Rohingya refugees to Bangladesh, Indonesia, Malaysia, Thailand, and other countries in the region.[134] Transnational criminal groups in Southeast Asia have formed to prey on Rohingya refugees, promising lucrative employment and deceiving them into boarding ships for Malaysia, only to keep them captive at sea or in trafficking camps along the Malaysia-Thailand border.[135] A number of victims have been killed, raped, and tortured. The criminals operating the vessels generate between $50 and $100 million annually, with traffickers earning an estimated $60,000 per ship.[136] Thai officials have been complicit in human trafficking rings, with the navy providing intercepted boats with supplies in exchange for their continuing on to Malaysia or Indonesia, thereby increasing the risk of trafficking.[137]

China's former one-child policy—which created a significant gender imbalance and a growing demand among unmarried Chinese men for brides—stimulated trafficking of foreign women into China, including from Myanmar.[138] These women are often sold into sexual slavery or forced labor and only allowed to leave China after giving birth. The price for a trafficked bride in China ranges from $3,000 to $13,000.[139]

The Tatmadaw, Myanmar's armed forces, have forcibly recruited children. Some are used as combatants, while others are forced to cook, clean, and serve as guards.[140] The International Labor Organization has been calling on Myanmar's government to eliminate the use of forced labor for over two decades. Although progress has been made, forced labor remains a persistent problem, particularly in conflict areas.[141]

NORTHERN TRIANGLE

The trafficking of Central American migrants demonstrates how criminals capitalize on the desperation of displaced populations and benefit from restrictive and punitive immigration policies. The Central American Northern Triangle countries of El Salvador, Guatemala, and Honduras are among the most violent countries in the world due to decades of political unrest, a proliferation of gangs, corrupt institutions, and a massive outflow of capital that deprives the region of funds for development and investment. Citizens contend with high levels of homicide, sexual and domestic violence, and extortion.[142] Authorities and law enforcement are often unable or unwilling to protect people from these crimes, with honest officials driven into exile. Many citizens flee the region and migrate north in search of stability and opportunity.[143]

In an effort to stem migrant flows from Central America, Trump has increased U.S. border security and implemented restrictive and punitive immigration policies. Measures include a zero-tolerance policy of criminally prosecuting people who irregularly enter the United States and the forced separation of families.[144] These immigration policies have offered smugglers, criminals, and traffickers an opportunity to capitalize on migrants' desperation to reach safety. Smugglers charge migrants exorbitant fees, and some leverage debt into forced labor or sexual exploitation.[145]

Large migrant flows and harsh immigration policies have presented drug trafficking organizations with an opportunity to generate revenue and expand into new areas of illicit activities. Los Zetas, the Mexican crime syndicate, has reportedly begun to hold migrants for ransom, in addition to forcing them into drug trafficking and sexually exploiting them.[146]

The Trump administration's crackdown on immigrants within the United States has hindered the ability of many immigrant survivors of human trafficking to receive protection and has allowed traffickers to operate with greater impunity. The Department of Homeland Security recently implemented a policy that requires officials—in far more cases than ever before—to begin deportation proceedings when applications for T visas are denied.[147] Processing times for T visas have increased since 2018, while approval rates have gone down.[148] This risk of deportation could prevent trafficking survivors from applying for visas and reporting their traffickers, making it more difficult for law enforcement officials to apprehend traffickers.

ENDNOTES

1. UN Office on Drugs and Crime, *Global Report on Trafficking in Persons 2018* (Vienna: United Nations, December 2018), 7, 10, http://unodc.org/documents/data-and -analysis/glotip/2018/GLOTiP_2018_BOOK_web_small.pdf.

2. International Labor Organization and Walk Free Foundation, *Global Estimates of Modern Slavery: Forced Labour and Forced Marriage* (Geneva: International Labor Organization, 2017), 9, http://ilo.org/wcmsp5/groups/public/---dgreports/---dcomm /documents/publication/wcms_575479.pdf.

3. "Trafficking in Persons, Especially Women and Children: Note by the Secretary-General," UN General Assembly, A/71/303 (August 5, 2016), http://reliefweb. int/sites/reliefweb.int/files/resources/N1625078.pdf; James Cockayne and Julie Oppermann, "Can We Sustain Peace by Fighting Human Trafficking in Conflict? Lessons From Libya," UN University Center for Policy Research, November 10, 2017, http://cpr.unu.edu/can-we-sustain-peace-by-fighting-human-trafficking-in-conflict -lessons-from-libya.html.

4. Resolution 2331, UN Security Council, S/Res/2331 (December 20, 2016), http:// securitycouncilreport.org/atf/cf/%7B65BFCF9B-6D27-4E9C-8CD3 -CF6E4FF96FF9%7D/s_res_2331.pdf.

5. Human Rights Watch, *Hopes Betrayed: Trafficking of Women and Girls to Post-Conflict Bosnia and Herzegovina for Forced Prostitution* (Human Rights Watch: November 2002), http://hrw.org/reports/2002/bosnia/Bosnia1102.pdf; Sarah E. Mendelson, *Barracks and Brothels: Peacekeepers and Human Trafficking in the Balkans* (Washington, DC: Center for Strategic and International Studies, February 2005), http://csis-prod.s3.amazonaws.com /s3fs-public/legacy_files/files/media/csis/pubs/0502_barracksbrothels.pdf.

6. International Labor Organization, *Profits and Poverty: The Economics of Forced Labour* (Geneva: International Labor Organization, 2014), 13, http://ilo.org/wcmsp5/groups /public/---ed_norm/---declaration/documents/publication/wcms_243391.pdf.

7. Nikita Malik, *Trafficking Terror: How Modern Slavery and Sexual Violence Fund Terrorism* (London: Henry Jackson Society, 2017), http://henryjacksonsociety.org/wp -content/uploads/2017/10/HJS-Trafficking-Terror-Report-web.pdf.

8. Sarah E. Mendelson, "Outsourcing Oppression: Trafficked Labor From North Korea," *Foreign Affairs*, May 28, 2015, http://foreignaffairs.com/articles/north-korea/2015-05 -28/outsourcing-oppression; "2019 Trafficking in Persons Report: Democratic People's Republic of Korea," U.S. Department of State (June 20, 2019), http://state.gov/reports /2019-trafficking-in-persons-report-2/democratic-peoples-republic-of-korea.

9. UN Office on Drugs and Crime, *Global Report on Trafficking in Persons 2018*.

10. "Human Trafficking," UN Office on Drugs and Crime, 2019, http://unodc.org/unodc /en/human-trafficking/what-is-human-trafficking.html.

11. James Cockayne and Summer Walker, *Fighting Human Trafficking in Conflict: 10 Ideas for Action by the United Nations Security Council* (New York: UN University, September 2016), http://collections.unu.edu/eserv/UNU:5780/UNUReport_Pages.pdf.

12. Malik, *Trafficking Terror*.

13. Charles Anthony Smith and Heather M. Smith, "Human Trafficking: The Unintended Effects of United Nations Intervention," *International Political Science Review* 32, no. 2 (2011): 125–45, http://journals.sagepub.com/doi/abs/10.1177/0192512110371240; Sam R. Bell et al., "U.N. Peacekeeping Forces and the Demand for Sex Trafficking," *International Studies Quarterly* 62, no. 3 (2018): 643–55, http://academic.oup.com /isq/article-abstract/62/3/643/5076386; Charles Anthony-Smith and Brandon Miller- de la Cuesta, "Human Trafficking in Conflict Zones: The Role of Peacekeepers in the Formation of Networks," *Human Rights Review* 12, no. 3 (2011): 287–99, http://link .springer.com/article/10.1007/s12142-010-0181-8.

14. Agnes Constante, "Who Are the 'Comfort Women,' and Why Are U.S.-Based Memorials for Them Controversial?" NBC, May 7, 2019, http://nbcnews.com/news /asian-america/who-are-comfort-women-why-are-u-s-based-memorials-n997656.

15. Paisley Dodds, "AP Exclusive: UN Child Sex Ring Left Victims but No Arrests," Associated Press, April 12, 2017, http://apnews.com /e6ebc331460345c5abd4f57d77f535c1; Edith M. Lederer, "UN Report: Sex Abuse in UN Peacekeeping Drops, Up Elsewhere," Associated Press, March 18, 2019, http:// apnews.com/8532c54fcc19462392bf2ae94a01e8f4.

16. Julia Zulver, "At Venezuela's Border With Colombia, Women Suffer Extraordinary Levels of Violence," *Washington Post*, February 26, 2019, http://washingtonpost.com /politics/2019/02/26/venezuelas-border-with-colombia-women-suffer-extraordinary -levels-violence.

17. U.S. Department of State, *Trafficking in Persons Report: June 2019* (Washington, DC: U.S. Department of State, 2019), http://state.gov/wp-content/uploads/2019/06/2019 -Trafficking-in-Persons-Report.pdf.

18. "Report on the Human Rights Situation of Migrants and Refugees in Libya," UN Support Mission in Libya and UN Office of the High Commissioner for Human Rights, December 19, 2018, http://ohchr.org/Documents/Countries/LY /InfographicsMigrationReport.pdf.

19. "Report of the Secretary-General on Conflict-Related Sexual Violence," UN Security Council, S/2018/250, March 23, 2018, ¶ 76, http://undocs.org/S/2018/250.

20. UN Office on Drugs and Crime, *Trafficking in Persons in the Context of Armed Conflict*

(Vienna: United Nations, December 2018), http://reliefweb.int/sites/reliefweb.int/files
/resources/GloTIP2018_BOOKLET_2_Conflict.pdf.

21. UNEP-MONUSCO-OSESG, *Experts' Background Report on Illegal Exploitation and
Trade in Natural Resources Benefitting Organized Criminal Groups and Recommendations
on MONUSCO's Role in Fostering Stability and Peace in Eastern DR Congo* (UNEP
-MONUSCO-OSESG, April 15, 2015), http://postconflict.unep.ch/publications
/UNEP_DRCongo_MONUSCO_OSESG_final_report.pdf; Diane Taylor, "Congo
Rape Victims Face Slavery in Gold and Mineral Mines," *Guardian*, September 2, 2011,
http://theguardian.com/world/2011/sep/02/congo-women-face-slavery-mines.

22. Sarah Craggs et al., "Responding to Human Trafficking and Exploitation in Times
of Crisis: Reducing the Vulnerabilities of Migrants in Preparedness, Response and
Recovery Efforts," Migrants in Countries in Crisis Initiative, January 2016, http://
micicinitiative.iom.int/sites/default/files/resource_pub/docs/trafficking_issue_brief
_final.pdf.

23. International Labor Organization and Walk Free Foundation, *Global Estimates of
Modern Slavery.*

24. "Trafficking in Persons, Especially Women and Children," UN General Assembly.

25. U.S. Department of State, *Trafficking in Persons Report: June 2019*; Syed Zain Al-
Mahmood, "Palm-Oil Migrant Workers Tell of Abuses on Malaysian Plantations," *Wall
Street Journal*, July 26, 2015, http://wsj.com/articles/palm-oil-migrant-workers-tell-of
-abuses-on-malaysian-plantations-1437933321.

26. "Children and Armed Conflict: Report of the Secretary-General," UN General
Assembly, A/72/865–S/2018/465 (May 16, 2018), http://undocs.org/s/2018/465;
"Children and Armed Conflict: Report of the Secretary-General," UN General
Assembly, A/72/361–S/2017/821 (August 24, 2017), http://undocs.org/A/72/361.

27. "Children and Armed Conflict: Report of the Secretary-General," UN General
Assembly Security Council, A/70/836–S/2016/360 (April 20, 2016), http://reliefweb
.int/sites/reliefweb.int/files/resources/N1611119.pdf; "Children and Armed Conflict:
Report of the Secretary-General," UN General Assembly, A/72/865–S/2018/465
(May 16, 2018), http://undocs.org/s/2018/465.

28. "Uganda: Child Soldiers at the Centre of Mounting Humanitarian Crisis," UN
Information Service, http://unis.unvienna.org/documents/unis/ten_stories/01uganda
.pdf; "LRA Child Soldiers Highly Traumatised," *New Humanitarian*, March 15, 2004,
http://thenewhumanitarian.org/news/2004/03/15/lra-child-soldiers-highly-traumatised.

29. Jo Becker, "A Better US List of Countries Using Child Soldiers: State Department
Restores Burma and Iraq to Its Annual List of Violators," Human Rights Watch, June 29,
2018, http://hrw.org/news/2018/06/29/better-us-list-countries-using-child-soldiers.

30. "Children and Armed Conflict: Report of the Secretary-General," UN General
Assembly Security Council, A/70/836–S/2016/360 (April 20, 2016), http://reliefweb
.int/sites/reliefweb.int/files/resources/N1611119.pdf.

31. "Child Soldiers Global Report 2008: Summary," Coalition to Stop the Use of Child
Soldiers, 2008, http://hrw.org/legacy/pub/2008/children/Child_Soldiers_Global
_Report_Summary.pdf; Human Rights Watch, *"We'll Kill You if You Cry": Sexual*

Violence in the Sierra Leone Conflict (New York: Human Rights Watch, January 16, 2003), http://hrw.org/report/2003/01/16/well-kill-you-if-you-cry/sexual-violence-sierra-leone-conflict; Human Rights Watch, *How to Fight, How to Kill: Child Soldiers in Liberia* (New York: Human Rights Watch, February 2, 2014), http://hrw.org/report/2004/02/02/how-fight-how-kill/child-soldiers-liberia; Jan Goodwin, "Sierra Leone Is No Place to Be Young," *New York Times,* February 14, 1999, http://nytimes.com/1999/02/14/magazine/sierra-leone-is-no-place-to-be-young.html.

32. Jason Warner and Hilary Matfess, *Exploding Stereotypes: The Unexpected Operational and Demographic Characteristics of Boko Haram's Suicide Bombers* (West Point: Combating Terrorism Center at West Point, U.S. Military Academy, August 2017), http://ctc.usma.edu/app/uploads/2017/08/Exploding-Stereotypes-1.pdf.

33. Yesica Fisch, "ISIS Starved Yazidi Children and Told Them They Could Eat in Paradise if They Carried Out Suicide Bombings," *Independent*, May 11, 2017, http://independent.co.uk/news/world/middle-east/isis-yazidi-children-syria-iraq-starved-suicide-bombings-eat-in-paradise-a7729581.html; Caroline Mortimer, "Isis Has Abducted Up to 400 Yazidi Children and Could Be Using Them as Suicide Bombers," *Independent*, January 14, 2016, http://independent.co.uk/news/world/middle-east/isis-has-abducted-up-to-400-yazidi-children-and-could-be-using-them-as-suicide-bombers-a6811876.html.

34. "Report of the Special Rapporteur on Trafficking in Persons, Especially Women and Children," Human Rights Council, UN General Assembly, A/HRC/32/41 (May 3, 2016), http://reliefweb.int/sites/reliefweb.int/files/resources/G1609048.pdf.

35. UN Office on Drugs and Crime, *Global Report on Trafficking in Persons in the Context of Armed Conflict*, 12.

36. David D. Kirkpatrick, "On the Front Line of the Saudi War in Yemen: Child Soldiers From Darfur," *New York Times*, December 28, 2018, http://nytimes.com/2018/12/28/world/africa/saudi-sudan-yemen-child-fighters.html.

37. Joana Cook and Gina Vale, *From Daesh to "Diaspora": Tracing the Women and Minors of Islamic State* (London: International Centre for the Study of Radicalisation, Department of War Studies, King's College London, 2018), http://icsr.info/wp-content/uploads/2018/07/ICSR-Report-From-Daesh-to-%E2%80%98Diaspora%E2%80%99-Tracing-the-Women-and-Minors-of-Islamic-State.pdf; Lizzie Dearden, "Missing Syria Girls: Parents Must 'Keep Passports Under Lock and Key' to Stop Children Joining ISIS," *Independent*, February 23, 2015, http://independent.co.uk/news/uk/crime/missing-syria-girls-parents-must-keep-passports-under-lock-and-key-to-stop-children-joining-isis-10065617.html.

38. Cockayne and Walker, *Fighting Human Trafficking in Conflict*; UN Office on Drugs and Crime, *Countering Trafficking in Persons in Conflict Situations* (Vienna: United Nations, 2018), http://unodc.org/documents/human-trafficking/2018/17-08776_ebook-Countering_Trafficking_in_Persons_in_Conflict_Situations.pdf; "Trafficking in Persons, Especially Women and Children," UN General Assembly.

39. "Assessment Toolkit: Trafficking in Persons for the Purpose of Organ Removal," UN Office on Drugs and Crime, 2015, http://unodc.org/documents/human-trafficking/2015/UNODC_Assessment_Toolkit_TIP_for_the_Purpose_of_Organ_Removal.pdf.

40. Hannah Roberts, "Migrants Are Being Forced to Sell Their Organs to Pay for Being Trafficked From Africa to Europe," *Daily Mail*, October 13, 2014, http://dailymail.co.uk /news/article-2790949/migrants-forced-sell-organs-pay-trafficked-africa-europe.html.

41. Nancy Scheper-Hughes, "Organ Trafficking During Times of War and Political Conflict," International Affairs Forum, http://ia-forum.org/Files/HDSQLC.pdf; Louise Shelley, *Dark Commerce: How a New Illicit Economy Is Threatening Our Future* (Princeton: Princeton University Press, 2018), chapter 6; Alex Forsyth, "Meeting an Organ Trafficker Who Preys on Syrian Refugees," BBC, April 25, 2017, http://bbc.com /news/magazine-39272511.

42. Warren Strobel, Jonathan Landay, and Phil Stewart, "Exclusive: Islamic State Sanctioned Organ Harvesting in Document Taken in U.S. Raid," Reuters, December 24, 2015, http://reuters.com/article/us-usa-islamic-state-documents-idUSKBN0U805R20151225; "First Responders' Toolbox: International Partnerships Among Public Health, Private Sector, and Law Enforcement Necessary to Mitigate ISIS's Organ Harvesting for Terrorist Funding," U.S. Joint Counterterrorism Assessment Team, May 11, 2017, http://dni.gov/files/NCTC/documents/jcat/firstresponderstoolbox/First-Responders -Toolbox---International-Partnerships-Among-Public-Health-Private-Sector-and-Law .pdf; Ray Sanchez, "United Nations Investigates Claim of ISIS Organ Theft," CNN, February 19, 2015, http://cnn.com/2015/02/18/middleeast/isis-organ-harvesting-claim; Anne Speckhard, "ISIS Defector Reports on the Sale of Organs Harvested From ISIS- Held 'Slaves,'" *Huffington Post*, January 1, 2016, http://huffpost.com/entry/isis-defector -reports-on-sale-of-organs_b_8897708; "Trafficking in Persons, Especially Women and Children," UN General Assembly.

43. Shelley, *Dark Commerce*, chapter 6.

44. Channing May, *Transnational Crime and the Developing World* (Washington, DC: Global Financial Integrity, March 2017), 29, http://gfintegrity.org/wp-content/uploads /2017/03/Transnational_Crime-final.pdf.

45. Shelley, *Dark Commerce*, chapter 6.

46. UN Office on Drugs and Crime, *Global Report on Trafficking in Persons in the Context of Armed Conflict.*

47. Jean Friedman-Rudovsky, "The Women Who Bear the Scars of Sierra Leone's Civil War," *Telegraph*, November 16, 2013, http://telegraph.co.uk/news/worldnews /africaandindianocean/sierraleone/10450619/The-women-who-bear-the-scars-of -Sierra-Leones-civil-war.html; Gregory Warner, "Nigerian Abductions Part of a Terrible Pattern in African Conflicts," WBUR, May 17, 2014, http://wbur.org/npr /313144946/nigerian-abductions-part-of-a-terrible-pattern-in-african-conflicts.

48. Rukmini Callimachi, "ISIS Enshrines a Theology of Rape," *New York Times,* August 13, 2015, http://nytimes.com/2015/08/14/world/middleeast/isis-enshrines-a-theology -of-rape.html.

49. UN Office on Drugs and Crime, *Global Report on Trafficking in Persons in the Context of Armed Conflict.*

50. Scholars refer to this practice as a "dual-use crime." *Exploring the Financial Nexus of Terrorism, Drug Trafficking, and Organized Crime, Hearing Before the Terrorism and Illicit Finance Subcommittee, House Financial Services Committee*, 115th Congress (2018)

(statement of Louise Shelley, Professor and Chair at George Mason University's Schar School of Policy and International Affairs), http://financialservices.house.gov/uploadedfiles/03.20.2018_louise_shelley_testimony.pdf; Cockayne and Walker, *Fighting Human Trafficking in Conflict.*

51. Malik, *Trafficking Terror.*

52. Callimachi, "ISIS Enshrines a Theology of Rape."

53. "Letter Dated 27 October 2014 From the Chair of the Security Council Committee Pursuant to Resolutions 1267 (1999) and 1989 (2011) Concerning Al-Qaida and Associated Individuals and Entities Addressed to the President of the Security Council," UN Security Council, S/2-14/770, http://refworld.org/docid/558bac664.html.

54. Mausi Segun and Samer Muscati, *"Those Terrible Weeks in Their Camp": Boko Haram Violence Against Women and Girls in Northeast Nigeria* (New York: Human Rights Watch, October 27, 2014), http://hrw.org/report/2014/10/27/those-terrible-weeks-their-camp/boko-haram-violence-against-women-and-girls.

55. Warner and Matfess, *Exploding Stereotypes.*

56. "Identifying and Exploring the Nexus Between Human Trafficking, Terrorism, and Terrorism Financing," Counter-Terrorism Committee Executive Directorate, UN Security Council, http://un.org/sc/ctc/wp-content/uploads/2019/02/HT-terrorism-nexus-CTED-report.pdf.

57. Jane Arraf, "Freed From ISIS, Yazidi Mothers Face Wrenching Choice: Abandon Kids or Never Go Home," NPR, May 9, 2019, http://npr.org/2019/05/09/721210631/freed-by-isis-yazidi-mothers-face-wrenching-choice-abandon-kids-or-never-go-home; "Yazidis to Accept ISIL Rape Survivors, but Not Their Children," Al Jazeera, April 29, 2019, http://aljazeera.com/news/2019/04/yazidis-accept-survivors-isil-rape-children-190428164100751.html.

58. "Report of the Secretary General on Conflict-Related Sexual Violence," UN Security Council.

59. Organization for Economic Cooperation and Development (OECD), *Trafficking in Persons and Corruption: Breaking the Chain,* OECD Public Governance Reviews (Paris: OECD, December 9, 2016), http://oecd-ilibrary.org/docserver/9789264253728-en.pdf; Council of Europe Programme Against Corruption and Organised Crime in South-Eastern Europe, *Trafficking in Human Beings and Corruption* (Strasbourg, France: Council of Europe, September 30, 2002), http://lastradainternational.org/lsidocs/297%20Trafficking%20and%20Corruption%20(PACO).pdf.

60. Jacob Townsend and Hayder Mili, "Human Smuggling and Trafficking: An International Terrorist Security Risk?," *CTC Sentinel* 1, no. 6 (May 2008), https://ctc.usma.edu/app/uploads/2010/06/Vol1Iss6-Art4.pdf.

61. June S. Beittel, *Mexico: Organized Crime and Drug Trafficking Organizations* (Congressional Research Service, July 3, 2018), http://fas.org/sgp/crs/row/R41576.pdf.

62. Cynthia J. Arnson and Eric L. Olson, eds., *Organized Crime in Central America: The Northern Triangle* (Washington, DC: Latin American Program, Woodrow Wilson International Center for Scholars, September 2011), http://wilsoncenter.org/sites/default/files/LAP_single_page.pdf.

63. Rune Henriksen and Sasha Jesperson, "Why Is Nigeria a Hub for Human Trafficking," Delta 8.7, October 11, 2018, http://delta87.org/2018/10/why-nigeria-hub-human-trafficking.

64. Thin Lei Win, "Italian Dream Over, Trafficked Nigerian Sets Sights on Home," Reuters, February 28, 2019, http://reuters.com/article/us-italy-slavery-survivor-feature/italian-dream-over-trafficked-nigerian-sets-sights-on-home-idUSKCN1QI38L.

65. International Centre for Migration Policy Development, *Targeting Vulnerabilities: The Impact of the Syrian War and Refugee Situation on Trafficking in Persons. A Study of Syria, Turkey, Lebanon, Jordan and Iraq* (Vienna: International Centre for Migration Policy Development, December 2015), http://icmpd.org/fileadmin/ICMPD-Website/Anti-Trafficking/Targeting_Vulnerabilities_EN__SOFT_.pdf; "STOP Sex Trafficking of Children & Young People," ECPAT International, April 2016, http://ecpat.org/wp-content/uploads/2016/04/Factsheet_Middle_East.pdf.

66. Special Monitoring Mission to Ukraine, Organization for Security and Cooperation in Europe (OSCE), *Conflict-Related Displacement in Ukraine: Increased Vulnerabilities of Affected Populations and Triggers of Tensions Within Communities* (OSCE, July 2016), http://osce.org/ukraine-smm/261176; U.S. Department of State, *Trafficking in Persons Report: June 2018* (Washington, DC: U.S. Department of State, 2018), http://state.gov/wp-content/uploads/2019/01/282798.pdf.

67. "Forced Labor," U.S. Holocaust Memorial Museum, http://ushmm.org/collections/bibliography/forced-labor.

68. "Eritrea: Events of 2018," Human Rights Watch, http://hrw.org/world-report/2019/country-chapters/eritrea.

69. Zoe Holman, "The Living Hell of Being a Girl Soldier in Eritrea," *Vice*, August 30, 2017, http://vice.com/en_au/article/8xxb3a/the-living-hell-of-being-a-girl-soldier-in-eritrea; "Report of the Commission of Inquiry on Human Rights in Eritrea," UN General Assembly, A/HRC/32/47, May 9, 2016, http://documents-dds-ny.un.org/doc/UNDOC/GEN/G16/093/42/PDF/G1609342.pdf.

70. Matthew Zweig, "North Korea's Use of Slave Labor Will Limit Any Prospective Sanctions Relief," Foundation for Defense of Democracies, February 27, 2019, http://fdd.org/analysis/2019/02/27/north-koreas-use-of-slave-labor-will-limit-any-prospective-sanctions-relief; Mendelson, *Outsourcing Oppression*; "2018 Trafficking in Persons Report: Democratic People's Republic of Korea," U.S. Department of State, June 28, 2018, http://state.gov/reports/2018-trafficking-in-persons-report/democratic-peoples-republic-of-korea/#report-toc__section-5; Resolution 2397, UN Security Council, S/RES/2397 (2017), http://unscr.com/en/resolutions/doc/2397; "Fact Sheet: UN Security Council Resolution 2397 on North Korea," U.S. Mission to the United Nations, December 22, 2017, http://usun.usmission.gov/fact-sheet-un-security-council-resolution-2397-on-north-korea.

71. "What Is Forced Labour, Modern Slavery and Human Trafficking," International Labor Organization, http://ilo.org/global/topics/forced-labour/definition/lang--en/index.htm.

72. International Labor Organization and Walk Free Foundation, *Global Estimates of Modern Slavery: Forced Labour and Forced Marriage*, 11.

73. Resolution 2331, UN Security Council, S/RES/2331 (2016).

74. "Iraq: Understanding the Situation in Areas of Return—Findings From Sinjar," REACH, June 22, 2018, http://reach-initiative.org/what-we-do/news/iraq -understanding-the-situation-in-areas-of-return-findings-from-sinjar.

75. Charlie Dunmore and Dalal Mawad, "Yazidi Doctor Brings Former ISIS Captives' Souls Back to Life," UN High Commissioner for Refugees, January 16, 2019, http:// unhcr.org/en-us/news/stories/2019/1/5c3da9ed4/yazidi-doctor-brings-former-isis -captives-souls-life.html.

76. UN Office on Drugs and Crime, *Transnational Organized Crime in Central America and the Caribbean: A Threat Assessment*; "Guidance Note on Refugee Claims Relating to Victims of Organized Gangs," Division of International Protection, UN High Commissioner for Refugees, March 31, 2010, https://www.refworld.org/docid /4bb21fa02.html; "Women on the Run: First-Hand Accounts of Refugees Fleeing El Salvador, Guatemala, Honduras, and Mexico," UN High Commissioner for Refugees (October 2015), http://unhcr.org/5630f24c6.pdf.

77. "Trafficking in Persons, Especially Women and Children," UN General Assembly; Cockayne and Oppermann, "Can We Sustain Peace by Fighting Human Trafficking in Conflict."

78. "An Introduction to Human Trafficking: Vulnerability, Impact and Action," UN Office on Drugs and Crime (2008), http://unodc.org/documents/human-trafficking/An _Introduction_to_Human_Trafficking_-_Background_Paper.pdf; Charlotte Lindsey-Curtet, Florence Tercier Holst-Roness, and Letitia Anderson, "Addressing the Needs of Women Affected by Armed Conflict: An ICRC Guidance Document," International Committee of the Red Cross (ICRC), March 2004, http://icrc.org/eng/assets/files /other/icrc_002 _0840_women_guidance.pdf.

79. UN Office on Drugs and Crime, *Countering Trafficking in Persons in Conflict Situations* (Vienna: United Nations, 2018); "Trafficking in Persons, Especially Women and Children," UN General Assembly.

80. UN Office on Drugs and Crime, *Countering Trafficking in Persons in Conflict Situations*.

81. Joshua Fruth, "Anti-Money Laundering Controls Failing to Detect Terrorists, Cartels, and Sanctioned States," Reuters, March 14, 2018, http://reuters.com/article/bc-finreg -laundering-detecting/anti-money-laundering-controls-failing-to-detect-terrorists -cartels-and-sanctioned-states-idUSKCN1GP2NV.

82. "Issue Paper: The Role of Corruption in Trafficking in Persons," UN Office on Drugs and Crime (2011), http://unodc.org/documents/human-trafficking/2011/Issue_Paper _-_The_Role_of_Corruption_in_Trafficking_in_Persons.pdf.

83. "Issue Paper: The Role of Corruption in Trafficking in Persons," UN Office on Drugs and Crime.

84. Smith and Smith, "Human Trafficking: The Unintended Effects of United Nations Intervention"; Mendelson, *Barracks and Brothels*; Bell, et al., "U.N. Peacekeeping Forces and the Demand for Sex Trafficking."

85. "Central African Republic: Rape by Peacekeepers," Human Rights Watch, February 4, 2016, http://hrw.org/news/2016/02/04/central-african-republic-rape-peacekeepers; U.S. Department of State, Trafficking in Persons Report: June 2019; Bethany Allen-

Ebrahimian, "U.N. Peacekeepers Ran a Child Sex Ring in Haiti," *Foreign Policy,* April 14, 2017, http://foreignpolicy.com/2017/04/14/u-n-peacekeepers-ran-a-child-sex-ring-in-haiti.

86. UN Office on Drugs and Crime, *Countering Trafficking in Persons in Conflict Situations.*

87. Choe Sang-Hun, "South Korea Illegally Held Prostitutes Who Catered to G.I.s Decades Ago, Court Says," *New York Times,* January 20, 2017, http://nytimes.com/2017/01/20/world/asia/south-korea-court-comfort-women.html; Choe Sang-Hun, "Ex-Prostitutes Say South Korea and U.S. Enabled Sex Trade Near Bases," *New York Times,* January 7, 2009, http://nytimes.com/2009/01/08/world/asia/08korea.html; Kim Young-jin, "Outside US Bases, Former Bar Workers Fight Sex Trafficking," *Korea Times,* February 27, 2012, http://koreatimes.co.kr/www/news/nation/2012/02/116_105839.html.

88. Donna M. Hughes, Katherine Y. Chon, and Derek P. Ellerman, "Modern-Day Comfort Women: The U.S. Military, Transnational Crime, and the Trafficking of Women," *Violence Against Women* 13, no. 9 (2007), http://journals.sagepub.com/doi/10.1177/1077801207305218.

89. David Vine, "My Body Was Not Mine, but the US Military's: Inside the Disturbing Sex Industry Thriving Around America's Bases," *Politico,* November 3, 2015, http://politico.eu/article/my-body-was-not-mine-but-the-u-s-militarys.

90. Samantha T. Godec, "Between Rhetoric and Reality: Exploring the Impact of Military Humanitarian Intervention Upon Sexual Violence – Post-Conflict Sex Trafficking in Kosovo," International Committee of the Red Cross (March 2010), http://icrc.org/en/international-review/article/between-rhetoric-and-reality-exploring-impact-military-humanitarian; *Kosovo (Serbia & Montenegro): "So Does That Mean I Have Rights?" Protecting the Human Rights of Women and Girls Trafficked for Forced Prostitution in Kosovo* (Amnesty International, May 2004), http://amnesty.org/download/Documents/96000/eur700102004en.pdf; Anthony-Smith and Miller-de la Cuesta, "Human Trafficking in Conflict Zones"; Olivier Peyroux, "Trafficking in Human Beings in Conflict and Post-Conflict Situation," Caritas (June 2015), http://caritas.org/wordpress/wp-content/uploads/2015/06/RESEARCH-ACTION-Trafficking-in-human-beings-and-conflicts-EN-10-juin-2015.pdf.

91. Human Rights Watch, *"I Wanted to Lie Down and Die": Trafficking and Torture of Eritreans in Sudan and Egypt* (New York: Human Rights Watch, February 2014), http://hrw.org/report/2014/02/11/i-wanted-lie-down-and-die/trafficking-and-torture-eritreans-sudan-and-egypt.

92. Cam Simpson, "Iraq War Contractors Ordered to End Abuses," *Chicago Tribune,* April 24, 2006, http://chicagotribune.com/news/ct-xpm-2006-04-24-0604240221-story.html; U.S. Department of Justice, *Assessment of U.S. Government Efforts to Combat Trafficking in Persons in Fiscal Year 2006* (U.S. Department of Justice, September 2007), 18, http://justice.gov/archive/ag/annualreports/tr2007/assessment-of-efforts-to-combat-tip0907.pdf.

93. "Presidential Executive Order on Enforcing Federal Law With Respect to Transnational Criminal Organizations and Preventing International Trafficking," White House, February 9, 2017, http://whitehouse.gov/presidential-actions/presidential-executive-order-enforcing-federal-law-respect-transnational-criminal-organizations-preventing-international-trafficking.

94. Robbie Gramer, "U.S. Stopped Vital Foreign Aid Programs in the Name of Counter-Trafficking," *Foreign Policy,* June 26, 2019, http://foreignpolicy.com/2019/06/26/us-stopped-vital-foreign-aid-programs-in-name-of-counter-trafficking-trafficking-in-persons-report-aid-development-programs-humanitarian-organizations.

95. UN Office on Drugs and Crime, *2018 Global Report on Trafficking in Persons.*

96. "End Trafficking Campaign: The Sustainable Development Goals That Aim to End Human Trafficking," UNICEF USA, January 29, 2016, http://unicefusa.org/stories/sustainable-development-goals-aim-end-human-trafficking/29864.

97. Financial Action Task Force (FATF) and Asia/Pacific Group (APG) on Money Laundering, *Financial Flows From Human Trafficking* (Paris: FATF and APG, July 2018), http://fatf-gafi.org/media/fatf/content/images/Human-Trafficking-2018.pdf; FATF, *Money Laundering Risks Arising From Trafficking of Human Beings and Smuggling of Migrants* (Paris: FATF, July 2011), http://www.fatf-gafi.org/media/fatf/documents/reports/Trafficking%20in%20Human%20Beings%20and%20Smuggling%20of%20Migrants.pdf.

98. "Conflict-Related Sexual Violence: Report of the Secretary-General," UN Security Council, S/2019/280, March 29, 2019, http://undocs.org/en/S/2019/280.

99. Network of Global Agenda Councils Task Force on Human Trafficking, World Economic Forum, *Hedging Risk by Combating Human Trafficking: Insights From the Private Sector* (Geneva: World Economic Forum, December 2014), http://www3.weforum.org/docs/WEF_Human_Trafficking_Report_2015.pdf.

100. Christina Bain, "How Data Can Help Fight Human Trafficking," World Economic Forum, February 18, 2015, http://weforum.org/agenda/2015/02/how-data-can-help-fight-human-trafficking.

101. Kamala D. Harris, "The California Transparency in Supply Chains Act: A Resource Guide," California Department of Justice, 2015, http://oag.ca.gov/sites/all/files/agweb/pdfs/sb657/resource-guide.pdf; Modern Slavery Act 2015, c. 30, Part 6, Section 54, http://legislation.gov.uk/ukpga/2015/30/section/54/enacted.

102. "Section 314(a)," Financial Crimes Enforcement Network, U.S. Department of the Treasury, http://fincen.gov/section-314a.

103. George Turner, "Switzerland, USA and Cayman Top the 2018 Financial Secrecy Index," Tax Justice Network, January 30, 2018, http://taxjustice.net/2018/01/30/2018fsi.

104. Peter Bergen, et al., "Terrorism in America After 9/11: Part II. Who Are the Terrorists?" International Security Program, New America, http://newamerica.org/in-depth/terrorism-in-america/who-are-terrorists; "European Union Terrorism Situation and Trend Report 2019," EU Agency for Law Enforcement Cooperation (2019), http://www.europol.europa.eu/activities-services/main-reports/terrorism-situation-and-trend-report-2019-te-sat.

105. David Bier, "Extreme Vetting of Immigrants: Estimating Terrorism Vetting Failures," Policy Analysis no. 838, Cato Institute, April 17, 2018, http://cato.org/publications/policy-analysis/extreme-vetting-immigrants-estimating-terrorism-vetting-failures.

106. Alex Nowrasteh, "Syrian Refugees Don't Pose a Serious Security Threat," Cato Institute, November 18, 2015, http://cato.org/blog/syrian-refugees-dont-pose-serious-security-threat.

107. U.S. Government Accountability Office, *Oversight of Contractors' Use of Foreign Workers in High-Risk Environments Needs to Be Strengthened* (Washington, DC: U.S. Government Accountability Office, November 2014, http://gao.gov/products/GAO -15-102; *Force for Hire* (podcast), "Episode 11: Exploitation, Human Trafficking Rampant in Third-Country National Contracting," Stars and Stripes, June 12, 2019, http://stripes.com/podcasts/force-for-hire/episode-11-exploitation-human-trafficking -rampant-in-third-country-national-contracting-1.585727; "Evaluation of DoD Efforts to Combat Trafficking in Persons in Kuwait DODIG-2019-088," Department of Defense Office of Inspector General, June 13, 2019, http://dodig.mil/reports.html /Article/1874544/evaluation-of-dod-efforts-to-combat-trafficking-in-persons-in -kuwait-dodig-2019.

108. Cheryl Pellerin, "DARPA Program Helps to Fight Human Trafficking," Defense Media Agency, January 4, 2017, http://ctip.defense.gov/News/News-Stories/News-Display /Article/1418180/darpa-program-helps-to-fight-human-trafficking.

109. UN Office of Drugs and Crime and Dutch National Rapporteur on Trafficking in Human Beings and Sexual Violence Against Children, *Monitoring Target 16.2 of the United Nations Sustainable Development Goals* (UN Office of Drugs and Crime, November 2017), http://unodc.org/documents/research/UNODC-DNR_research _brief.pdf.

110. U.S. Department of State, *Trafficking in Persons Report: June 2019.*

111. "Iraq: ISIS Escapees Describe Systematic Rape: Yezidi Survivors in Need of Urgent Care," Human Rights Watch, April 14, 2015, http://hrw.org/news/2015/04/14/iraq -isis-escapees-describe-systematic-rape; UN High Commissioner For Human Rights UN Assistance Mission For Iraq—Human Rights Office, *A Call for Accountability and Protection: Yezidi Survivors of Atrocities Committed by ISIL* (United Nations, August 2016), http://uniraq.org/images/humanrights/UNAMI%20OHCHR_Report%20 Yezidi%20Survivors%20A%20Call%20for%20Justice_FINAL_12Aug2016.pdf.

112. Malik, *Trafficking Terror.*

113. UN Office on Drugs and Crime, *Countering Trafficking in Persons in Conflict Situations*; Jamie Dettmer, "Steeped in Martyrdom, Cubs of the Caliphate Groomed as Jihadist Legacy," Voice of America, July 6, 2016, http://voanews.com/world -news/middle-east-dont-use/steeped-martyrdom-cubs-caliphate-groomed-jihadist-legacy.

114. U.S. Department of State, *Trafficking in Persons Report: June 2019.*

115. Ann Knapp, *Human Trafficking in the Kurdistan Region of Iraq* (Seed Foundation, December 2018), http://seedkurdistan.org/Downloads/Trafficking/Anti_trafficking _report_EnglishSEED_2019_outlined_very_final_2132019.pdf.

116. Knapp, *Human Trafficking in the Kurdistan Region.*

117. Cockayne and Oppermann, "Can We Sustain Peace by Fighting Human Trafficking"; Mark Micallef, *The Human Conveyor Belt: Trends in Human Trafficking and Smuggling in Post-Revolution Libya* (Geneva: Global Initiative Against Transnational Organized Crime, March 2017), http://globalinitiative.net/wp-content/uploads/2017/03/GI -Human-Conveyor-Belt-Human-Smuggling-Libya-2017-.pdf.

118. Cockayne and Oppermann, "Can We Sustain Peace by Fighting Human Trafficking"; Tuesday Reitano and Mark Shaw, "Libya: The Politics of Power, Protection, Identity

and Illicit Trade," UN University Center for Policy Research (May 2017), http://i.unu .edu/media/cpr.unu.edu/attachment/2523 /Libya-The-Politics-of-Power-Protection -Identity-and-Illicit-Trade-02.pdf.

119. "UNHCR Dismayed as Traffickers, Smugglers Impersonate Staff in Libya Amid Clashes in Tripoli," UNHCR, September 8, 2018, http://unhcr.org/news/press/2018 /9/5b93c3924/unhcr-dismayed-traffickers-smugglers-impersonate-staff-libya-amid -clashes.html.

120. "Conflict-Related Sexual Violence: Report of the Secretary-General," UN Security Council, S/2019/280, March 29, 2019, http://undocs.org/en/S/2019/280.

121. "Letter Dated 5 September 2018 From the Panel of Experts on Libya Established Pursuant to Resolution 1973 (2011) Addressed to the President of the Security Council," UN Security Council, S/2018/812, http://undocs.org/S/2018/812.

122. Philip Obaji Jr., "When the Way Out of Boko Haram Is an Ancient Slave Route," *Daily Beast,* December 2, 2017, http://thedailybeast.com/when-the-way-out-of-boko-haram -is-an-ancient-slave-route.

123. "Letter Dated 5 September 2018," UN Security Council.

124. Patrick Wintour, "Refugees Report Brutal and Routine Sexual Violence in Libya," *Guardian,* March 25, 2019, http://theguardian.com/world/2019/mar/25/refugees -face-routine-sexual-violence-in-libyan-detention-centres-report.

125. Cockayne and Walker, "Fighting Human Trafficking in Conflict."

126. U.S. Department of State, *Trafficking in Persons Report: June 2019.*

127. Sally Hayden, "Fear and Despair Engulf Refugees in Libya's 'Market of Human Beings,'" *Guardian,* April 15, 2019, http://theguardian.com/global-development/2019/apr/15 /fear-and-despair-engulf-refugees-in-libyas-market-of-human-beings; Global Detention Project, *Immigration Detention in Libya: "A Human Rights Crisis"* (Geneva: Global Detention Project, August 2018), http://reliefweb.int/sites/reliefweb.int/files /resources/GDP-Immigration-Detention-Libya.pdf.

128. Peter Tinti, "Libya: Nearly There, but Never Further Away," Pulitzer Center, October 5, 2017, http://pulitzercenter.org/reporting/libya-nearly-there-never-further-away; Global Detention Project, *Immigration Detention in Libya.*

129. Nancy Porsia, "The Kingpin of Libya's Human Trafficking Mafia," *TRT World,* February 20, 2017, http://trtworld.com/magazine/libya-human-trafficking-mafia-in -zawiya-301505.

130. Selam Gebrekidan, "Special Report: Enslaved in Libya—One Woman's Extraordinary Escape from Islamic State," *Reuters,* August 18, 2016, http://reuters.com/article/us -europe-migrants-slave-special-report-idUSKCN10T137.

131. Gebrekidan, "Special Report: Enslaved in Libya."

132. U.S. Department of State, *Trafficking in Persons Report: June 2019.*

133. U.S. Department of State, *Trafficking in Persons Report: June 2018*; U.S. Department of State, *Trafficking in Persons Report: June 2019.*

134. Eleanor Albert and Andrew Chatzky, "The Rohingya Crisis," Council on Foreign Relations, last updated December 5, 2018, http://cfr.org/backgrounder/rohingya-crisis.

135. Human Rights Commission of Malaysia and Fortify Rights, *"Sold Like Fish": Crimes Against Humanity, Mass Graves, and Human Trafficking From Myanmar and Bangladesh to Malaysia From 2012 to 2015* (Human Rights Commission of Malaysia and Fortify Rights, March 2019), http://fortifyrights.org/downloads/Fortify%20Rights-SUHAKAM%20-%20Sold%20Like%20Fish.pdf.

136. Human Rights Commission of Malaysia and Fortify Rights, *"Sold Like Fish."*

137. Ryn Jirenuwat and Russell Goldman, "Dozens Found Guilty in Thailand in Human-Trafficking Case, *New York Times,* July 19, 2017, http://nytimes.com/2017/07/19/world/asia/thailand-human-trafficking-case.html; "Thailand: Trafficking Convictions Important Step Forward: Expand Prosecutions, Provide Protections for Rohingya Migrants," Human Rights Watch, July 24, 2017, http://hrw.org/news/2017/07/24/thailand-trafficking-convictions-important-step-forward.

138. Human Rights Watch, *"Give Us a Baby and We'll Let You Go": Trafficking of Kachin "Brides" From Myanmar to China* (New York: Human Rights Watch, March 2019), http://hrw.org/report/2019/03/21/give-us-baby-and-well-let-you-go/trafficking-kachin-brides-myanmar-china.

139. Human Rights Watch, *"Give Us a Baby and We'll Let You Go."*

140. "2017 Findings on the Worst Forms of Child Labor: Burma," U.S. Department of Labor, 2017, http://dol.gov/sites/default/files/documents/ilab/Burma.pdf.

141. "ILO Deputy Director-General Meets Myanmar Army Chief of General Staff to Discuss Forced Labour," International Labor Organization press release, September 20, 2018, http://ilo.org/yangon/press/WCMS_645336/lang--en/index.htm; Aubrey Belford and Soe Zeya Tun, "Forced Labor Shows Back-Breaking Lack of Reform in Myanmar Military," Reuters, July 2, 2015, http://reuters.com/article/us-myanmar-rohingya-forcedlabour/forced-labor-shows-back-breaking-lack-of-reform-in-myanmar-military-idUSKCN0PC2L720150702.

142. Rocio Cara Labrador and Danielle Renwick, "Central America's Violent Northern Triangle," Council on Foreign Relations, last updated June 26, 2018, http://cfr.org/backgrounder/central-americas-violent-northern-triangle.

143. Adriana Beltrán, "Children and Families Fleeing Violence in Central America," WOLA Advocacy for Human Rights in the Americas, February 21, 2017, http://wola.org/analysis/people-leaving-central-americas-northern-triangle.

144. "Statement From DHS Press Secretary on April Border Numbers," U.S. Department of Homeland Security press release, May 4, 2018, http://dhs.gov/news/2018/05/04/statement-dhs-press-secretary-april-border-numbers; Hillel R. Smith, "An Overview of U.S. Immigration Laws Regulating the Admission and Exclusion of Aliens at the Border," Congressional Research Service, November 27, 2018, http://fas.org/sgp/crs/homesec/LSB10150.pdf.

145. Jasmine Garsd, "In Central America, Human Smugglers Entrap Women in Sex Trafficking," *All Things Considered,* NPR, January 28, 2016, http://npr.org/2016/01/28/464744474/in-central-america-human-smugglers-entrap-women-in-sex-trafficking.

146. UN Office on Drugs and Crime, *Transnational Organized Crime in Central America and the Caribbean.*

147. "Notice to Appear Policy Memorandum," U.S. Citizenship and Immigration Services, last updated February 26, 2019, https://www.uscis.gov/legal-resources/notice-appear-policy-memorandum.

148. Jenna Krajeski, "Trump's Human Trafficking Record Is Fake News," *Foreign Policy,* June 20, 2019, http://foreignpolicy.com/2019/06/20/trumps-human-trafficking-record-is-fake-news/.

ACKNOWLEDGMENTS

This report was produced under the guidance of CFR's Advisory Committee on the Security Implications of Human Trafficking, a distinguished group of experts from the government, multilateral organizations, academia, and the private and public sectors. Over the past several months, members of this advisory committee have participated in meetings, reviewed drafts, and shared research and insights from their work. The report has been enhanced considerably by the expertise of this advisory group, and we are thankful for members' participation. The views expressed here and any errors are our own.

A special acknowledgment is extended to James M. Lindsay, CFR's director of studies, and Shannon O'Neil, CFR's vice president and deputy director of studies, for their support for this project, and to Joshua Kurlantzick, CFR senior fellow, for his partnership in this effort. We are grateful to Patricia Dorff and Julie Hersh for their review of previous drafts, and to Rebecca Turkington, Alexandra Bro, Rebecca Hughes, and Mallory Matheson for their excellent assistance in the production of this paper. U.S. officials also provided feedback that significantly contributed to the report.

This report was written under the auspices of the Women and Foreign Policy program, whose work on human trafficking, conflict, and security is supported by Humanity United (HU). The opinions expressed are those of the authors and do not necessarily reflect the views of HU.

Jamille Bigio
Rachel Vogelstein

ABOUT THE AUTHORS

Jamille Bigio is a senior fellow in the Women and Foreign Policy program at the Council on Foreign Relations. Previously, she was director for human rights and gender on the White House National Security Council staff and advised First Lady Michelle Obama on adolescent girls' education. From 2009 to 2013, Bigio was senior advisor to the U.S. ambassador-at-large for global women's issues at the Department of State and was detailed to the office of the undersecretary of defense for policy and the U.S. Mission to the African Union. Bigio led the interagency launch of the U.S. National Action Plan on Women, Peace, and Security, an effort for which she was recognized with the U.S. Department of State Superior Honor Award and the U.S. Department of Defense Secretary of Defense Honor Award. Bigio graduated from the University of Maryland and received her master's degree from the Harvard Kennedy School.

Rachel Vogelstein is the Douglas Dillon senior fellow and director of the Women and Foreign Policy program at the Council on Foreign Relations. From 2009 to 2012, Vogelstein was director of policy and senior advisor within the office of U.S. Secretary of State Hillary Clinton and represented the U.S. Department of State as a member of the White House Council on Women and Girls. Previously, Vogelstein was the director of the women and girls programs in the office of Hillary Clinton at the Clinton Foundation, where she oversaw the development of the No Ceilings initiative and provided guidance on domestic and global women's issues. Prior to joining the State Department, Vogelstein was senior counsel at the National Women's Law Center in Washington, DC, where she specialized in women's health and reproductive rights. Vogelstein is a recipient of the U.S. Department of State Superior Honor Award and a National Association of Women Lawyers award. She graduated from Barnard College and received a law degree from Georgetown Law School.

ADVISORY COMMITTEE
The Security Implications of Human Trafficking

Christina A. Bain
Babson College

James Cockayne
UN University

Jennifer Fowler
Brunswick Group

Nicholas D. Kristof
New York Times

Joshua Kurlantzick, *ex officio*
Council on Foreign Relations

Mark Lagon
Friends of the Global Fight Against AIDS, Tuberculosis and Malaria

Cindy McCain
McCain Institute

Sarah E. Mendelson
*Carnegie Mellon University;
Former U.S. Representative to the
UN Economic and Social Council*

Nadia Murad
*Nadia's Initiative;
UN Office on Drugs and Crime
Goodwill Ambassador for the
Dignity of Survivors of Human
Trafficking*

Stephen Rapp
*U.S. Holocaust Memorial Museum;
Former Ambassador-at-Large for
Global Criminal Justice*

Louise Shelley
George Mason University

Sherri Kraham Talabany
SEED Foundation

This report reflects the judgments and recommendations of the authors. It does not necessarily represent the views of members of the advisory committee, whose involvement should in no way be interpreted as an endorsement of the report by either themselves or the organizations with which they are affiliated.

www.ingramcontent.com/pod-product-compliance
Lightning Source LLC
Chambersburg PA
CBHW070817280326
41934CB00012B/3210

9 780876 097755